"If you've ever wondered what Jesus might say specifically to you, this is your book and you're going to love it! Andrew Farley presents the magnificent truth of the gospel in the form of a conversation—as though Jesus were talking directly to you, and you to Jesus. Your heart will open wide to your Savior as you marvel at his love for you. And there's nothing more life-changing than that!"

—Ralph Harris, author of
God's Astounding Opinion of You

"What a promise: there is another world, and it can start now, in this one. Read *Heaven Is Now* to discover hidden everyday reflections that can awaken your 'five spiritual senses' so that you can begin eternity now. This book is heaven-sent."

—Leonard Sweet, bestselling author, professor, and chief contributor to Sermons.com

"Andrew Farley has a unique and special understanding of grace. In *Heaven Is Now*, he articulates the depths of God's grace in a way that every believer can understand. This is the official grace handbook for Christians everywhere!"

—Darin Hufford, bestselling author of
The Misunderstood God

"Here is a gentleness that captures not only the content of Jesus's message but his loving heart and warmth as well. Within this invitation to experience heaven in the here and now, Farley offers the encouragement of a Good News that's much better than what Christians are usually taught. God's tenderness leaps from every page."

—David Gregory, bestselling author of
Dinner with a Perfect Stranger

HEAVEN IS NOW

HEAVEN **IS NOW**

awakening your five spiritual senses
to the wonders of grace

ANDREW **FARLEY**

BakerBooks

a division of Baker Publishing Group
Grand Rapids, Michigan

© 2012 by Andrew Farley

Published by Baker Books
a division of Baker Publishing Group
P.O. Box 6287, Grand Rapids, MI 49516-6287
www.bakerbooks.com

ISBN 978-0-8010-1482-6 (ITPE)

Printed in the United States of America

Library of Congress Cataloging-in-Publication Data
Farley, Andrew, 1972–
    Heaven is now : awakening your five spiritual senses to the wonders of grace / Andrew Farley.
        p.   cm.
    ISBN 978-0-8010-1438-3 (cloth)
    1. Senses and sensation—Religious aspects—Christianity. 2. Spirituality. 3. Heaven—Christianity. 4. Grace (Theology) I. Title.
BT741.3.F37 2012
248.4—dc23   2011042756

The diagram on page 96 is adapted from a 3-D model by Leslie Farley.

The internet addresses, email addresses, and phone numbers in this book are accurate at the time of publication. They are provided as a resource. Baker Publishing Group does not endorse them or vouch for their content or permanence.

In keeping with biblical principles of creation stewardship, Baker Publishing Group advocates the responsible use of our natural resources. As a member of the Green Press Initiative, our company uses recycled paper when possible. The text paper of this book is composed in part of post-consumer waste.

Published in association with the literary agency of Alive Communications, Inc., 7680 Goddard Street, Suite 200, Colorado Springs, CO 80920, alivecommunications.com.

12   13   14   15   16   17   18   7   6   5   4   3   2   1

To my wife, Katharine

CONTENTS

AWAKEN!

In 1998, my father was in a bad car accident. As he lay there in a coma in Fairfax County Hospital, a pastor arrived and tried to heal him. The pastor anointed him with oil, prayed for him, and tried to raise him from the dead. But my dad wouldn't have it. His limp body just lay there, lifeless.

Sometimes we want to change our circumstances. We want to manipulate the externals so that we can somehow feel better on the inside. We want to ask, even in Jesus's name, that things be different.

We want control.

But if you've lived more than a day, you've already figured out that it's not happening. We are *not* in control. Things happen, and we have no say in the matter. Clearly, we're not going to experience something different by controlling our circumstances. Hope must come from somewhere else. Hope must come from heaven *in the midst of* what earth presents us.

Any other hope is delusion.

INVITED TO HEAVEN

An early church writer spoke of this hope from heaven: "We have this hope as an anchor for the soul, firm and secure. It enters the inner sanctuary behind the curtain, where our forerunner, Jesus, has entered on our behalf" (Heb. 6:19–20). But Jesus never entered any inner sanctuary in the Jewish temple. He wasn't permitted behind the curtain. Here, the writer means *heaven itself*, where Jesus entered after his resurrection.

But there's more. Speaking of this heavenly sanctuary, the writer then claims that "*we* have confidence to enter the Most Holy Place by the blood of Jesus, by a new and living way" (Heb. 10:19–20). This too means heaven, but this time *we* are invited.

This invitation is not merely about a future in heaven. It's about awakening to a very present hope. Our God has set it up for today, and he invites us to enter in. Why does he bother with such a spectacular invitation?

Because heaven is *now*.

THE KINGDOM WITHIN

Heaven is *now*?

We're told that God "seated us with him in the heavenly realms" (Eph. 2:6), that "our citizenship is in heaven" (Phil. 3:20), and that we are "aliens and strangers" in this world (1 Pet. 2:11 NASB). We explain these away the best we can. We can't have our faith involving such ridiculous notions. After all, how can any of it really be true here and now in the midst of so much ugliness all around us?

The early church knew this ugliness. They saw it up close and personal as many of them were taken from their families, imprisoned, tortured, even killed. They were no strangers to trouble. Still, they insisted—heaven is *now*.

No, we can't know *all* of heaven here and now. It will take a lifetime and more to gather it in. But even if we only partially realize heaven's splendor on this side, it is still the sweetest form of life to embrace in the midst of all that earth throws our way.

I'm not making any promises that your circumstances will get better. Our circumstances are externals. This book is about what goes on *inside* of us in the midst of our circumstances, not outside or all around us. As Jesus put it, "The kingdom of God is *within* you" (Luke 17:21 NKJV).

Toward the Sky

We hear that heaven is now, and we wish to *feel* it. But our feelings come and go, as we travel from the heights of happiness to the depths of despair in seconds. We ride the roller coaster of the soul every day. So what if the real hope we have is not found in our feelings? Would that kind of hope be worth pursuing?

The way called faith brings this hope from heaven. We have the faith. We need only point it toward the sky. Let me tell you about someone who did.

Horatio Spafford was a wealthy lawyer in Chicago. You could look down a Chicago street and it was nearly all his. Horatio had millions. He also had a lovely wife and four beautiful daughters.

One day, a fire swept through Chicago, destroying nearly all Horatio owned. Two years later he sent his family on vacation across the ocean to England. But their ship went down, and only Horatio's wife survived. He received a telegram from her that read "Saved alone."

Horatio then sailed to England to meet up with his wife, so they could grieve together. On his way, he sat in the hull of that ship and wrote the song, "It Is Well with My Soul."

Horatio lost almost everything. He lost his four daughters and his fortune. His life had turned into tragedy. How could he write that it was well with him? Was he delusional?

As the lyrics of his song reveal, the condition of his soul didn't reflect the circumstances around him. His wellness came as he angled his soul toward heaven. He was awakened to heaven's love. He was reflecting heaven's life. He perceived these with spiritual senses, despite what his physical senses were telling him.

Our Five Spiritual Senses

So how exactly do we experience heaven here and now? We already possess the senses we need to take in heaven's goodness (Heb. 5:14 NASB). We need only have these senses awakened:

- We can *feel* the freedom of God's grace.
- We can *hear* the Spirit bearing witness.
- We can *see* the finished work of Jesus.
- We can *smell* the fragrant aroma of Christ.
- We can *taste* the goodness of the Lord.

Through these five spiritual senses, we experience heaven on this side. We don't see heaven with the natural eye. But by faith we enter into all that it means to be raised and seated with Christ (Eph. 2:6), and we are awakened to heaven's grace.

In preparation for writing this book, I spent many months reading through God's Word, over and over, to take in the big picture. All the while, I was asking: What is heaven trying to tell us?

Here is our first message from heaven.

HEAVEN SPEAKS

My heart's desire is that you rest in me. The heavenly promises I have made to you are designed to give you peace, even in the most violent of storms.

Sometimes you plead with me for a circumstance to change. You ask again and again that it be taken away. My heart longs for you to see more fully how my grace is sufficient for you, even in this. For my power is made perfect in the midst of your weakness.

Through my finished work, I have made you clean and close to me, and you are invited to live in a spiritual seventh day, relaxing in me. But to rest in me takes work. It's not the kind of work you're used to but a very different kind of work. I'm asking you to dig deeper into all that I've done for you so that you can more fully celebrate it, even when outwardly there seems only cause for pain.

I long for you to awaken to the goodness of my grace. As you discover the heights and depths of my love for you, you will experience relationship with me like you never imagined possible.

I love you, and I long for you to know me as I truly am.

Jesus

Awakening TO HEAVEN

Thank you, Jesus, for inviting me to rest. I welcome the adventure of awakening to your grace. I acknowledge that I have no real strength within myself. Instead, I am here, transparent before you, glorying in my weaknesses so that your power may rest on me. I love you, Jesus. And I want to learn more of your goodness toward me so that you can be my anchor, my stability in any storm.

Heaven Speaks inspired by Hebrews 3:15; 4:9–11; 6:19; John 14:27; 16:33; 2 Corinthians 12:8–10; Ephesians 3:18.

FEEL
THE FREEDOM
OF GRACE

**It is for freedom that
Christ has set us free.**

Galatians 5:1

1

Skydivers carry an extra parachute. You know, just in case. After all, anything can happen up there. Who's to say the first parachute is going to work? So in the event of a wardrobe malfunction, they're ready to deploy plan B.

Now imagine that I invite you to go skydiving with me, but only under one condition: you can't carry a backup chute. Would you take me up on that offer?

For some of us, skydiving is scary enough on its own, much less without a backup plan! It takes a gutsy person to put all their stock in the one chute, trusting they won't fall to their doom.

It's the same way with heaven's grace, our trusty parachute. God invites us on the skydiving adventure of a lifetime. He invites us to trust his way of grace that will never fail. But when we discover that his invitation means we're supposed to forego the "backup chute" of self-effort, our knees start knocking: "Are you *sure* it's safe?"

THE BUZZWORD

Grace is a word we've heard thousands of times in our lives, especially in church. We think grace means we aren't punished when we should be. We think grace is there to pick us up when we've fallen.

While these are true, I've found that grace has no depth to it apart from a solid understanding of what heaven calls "the new covenant." Without an awakening to this covenant, our understanding of grace will be limited to what we know or feel is true about the character of God. We will walk in grace only to the degree that we *feel* God is gracious toward us. The result is that our view of God's grace may be way off base without us even realizing it.

But through the new covenant, heaven defines grace in *precise* terms for us. When we have our senses awakened to the new covenant, we perceive exactly how God demonstrated his grace toward us. And it's grace we can sink our teeth into.

HEAVEN'S PERFECT STANDARD

For years, I only knew "new covenant" as the name of the church down the street—New Covenant Bible Church or New Covenant Chapel of God. So what exactly is the new covenant? And how does it help us feel the freedom of heaven's grace? To answer these, we'd better start with the *old* covenant.

The old covenant was the Jewish law that God gave to Israel. It consisted of about 613 dos and don'ts. Scripture tells us that the law never saved anyone (Rom. 3:20; Gal. 2:16; 3:21). The law was intended only as a shadow, a picture of the Christ to come (Col. 2:17; Heb. 10:1). It's true that many looked to the law for hope of salvation, but in the end they found that the law only brought condemnation and death (2 Cor. 3:7).

Today, the law serves as a tool for *un*believers (1 Tim. 1:8–11). It makes us humans aware of our sin problem (Rom. 3:19–20). Within ourselves, we have no adequate response to heaven's perfect standard. The law's strict demands make it quite clear that we fall short:

> For if a law had been given that could impart life, then righteousness would certainly have come by the law. *But Scripture has locked up everything under the control of sin*, so that what was promised, being given through faith in Jesus Christ, might be given to those who believe. (Gal. 3:21–22)

The law doesn't encourage or praise us. Being under law is like being married to an abusive perfectionist. Even if you please your spouse and only stumble in one way here or there, they treat you as if you're a good-for-nothing, sorry excuse for a human being. They act like you're guilty of disregarding *everything* they've ever asked of you: "whoever keeps the whole law and stumbles in one point is guilty of all" (James 2:10).

Being under law is like being under a curse, because "cursed is everyone who does not continue to do *everything* written in the Book of the Law" (Gal. 3:10). The law is an all-or-nothing proposition. If anyone invests in the old way of the law, they are "obligated to obey the *whole* law" (5:3).

THE COVENANT CONVENTION

At the first religious convention in history, Moses trotted down the mountain with stone tablets in hand. He read everything aloud to the people of Israel. The Israelites signed on the dotted line, saying, "We will do everything" (Exod. 24:7). But the convention was a bust. The old covenant story is one of broken promise after broken promise to God.

Heaven wasn't taken by surprise. God never intended Israel (or anyone!) to be able to keep the law. The law wasn't designed to bring success. No, the law came into the picture so that sin would *increase* (Rom. 5:20), not decrease.

HEAVEN'S NEW WAY

Heaven wanted earth to see that, apart from divine intervention, there was no real hope. Then, at the appointed time, the powers of heaven ushered in a new covenant that put *God's faithfulness to himself* on display: "since He could swear by no one greater, He swore by Himself" (Heb. 6:13 NASB).

God swore to himself that Jesus would be our priest forever (7:21–22). He promised that he would never leave us nor forsake us (13:5). He promised to be faithful to himself. He became our guarantor of a better covenant (7:22).

Here's what God himself says about this new covenant: "It will *not be like the covenant* I made with their ancestors . . . because they did not remain faithful to my covenant. . . . I will put my laws in their *minds* and write them on their *hearts*. I will be their God, and they will be my people" (Heb. 8:9–10).

Did you notice what the new covenant is all about? It's about heaven's solution to our faithlessness. It's about God rigging everything by placing Christ's desires in our hearts and minds. It's about God's commitment to be our God forever. Here, God is the initiator. All we *can* do is respond with belief and a "thank you."

CELEBRATE SECURITY!

Most Christians who worry about their eternal security have imagined some scenario in which they commit a particularly heinous sin or get caught in a series of sins. Then their lack of faithfulness takes center stage in God's decision to axe them. But through the new covenant, heaven is announcing that the work of Jesus is now on display at center stage.

When we place our faithfulness to God in the limelight and believe it to be a potential cause for loss of salvation, we are confusing the new covenant with the old. The whole point of the new way is to eliminate the faithfulness problem under the old way, "because they did not remain faithful" (Heb. 8:9). Heaven declares that "if we are faithless, he remains faithful, for he cannot disown himself" (2 Tim. 2:13). To disown us would be to disown himself, because he resides in us forever!

Heaven wants us to celebrate our security. And when we allow the work of Jesus to take center stage in our lives, we adopt a heavenly perspective in the midst of our earthly circumstances.

Here's heaven's next message to us.

I brought the law into the picture so that Israel would sense their sinfulness apart from me. To this day, my law holds everyone accountable to a standard they cannot possibly meet. My law silences all who truly confront it. There is simply no response after encountering its perfect standard, because it curses you for not keeping all of it.

But I have called you to feel the glorious freedom of my grace. If you are in me and I am in you, I have freed you from the all-or-nothing curse of the law. The law is not your ticket to life in me. You've been transferred out of the reign of law and into my kingdom of grace.

By faith you have received the promised inheritance of my Spirit. This promise was given long before the law came on the scene. I wanted to show you that, entirely apart from law, you are made whole in me.

Since the day I came to live in you, I've been leading you toward freedom. I've called you away from rules and regulations to enjoy an exhilarating new motivation—my Spirit in you.

My new covenant is not about how much commitment or dedication you are able to muster. I have already witnessed the best efforts any humans can make. No, this new covenant is about my best efforts on the cross and through the resurrection.

You are called to enjoy the fruit of my labor. This is what makes the glory of my new way more brilliant than the old. You are as safe as I am, and our Father will never disown us.

I will always love you.

Jesus

Awakening TO HEAVEN

Thank you, Jesus, for calling me out to the freedom of your grace. I can see the purpose of the old way, and I am so grateful for the new! Thank you for rescuing me from an impossible standard and making me perfect through your sacrifice. You have delivered me from the curse of the law and shared your very self with me by your Spirit. Any false hopes I had under an achieving system can now be replaced with a genuine hope in you. Thank you for walking with me in this journey and holding me tightly along the way.

I love you too.

Heaven Speaks inspired by Romans 3:19; 5:20; 6:14; 7:7; Galatians 3:10, 17, 21; 5:1, 18; James 2:10; Hebrews 4:10; 6:13; 1 John 4:17.

2

In 1920, alcohol sales became prohibited throughout the United States. Within a matter of weeks, people all over the country were purchasing portable alcohol stills and large quantities of fermentable foods to begin "bootlegging." Organized smuggling from Canada quickly developed, and alcohol was sold from ship to ship as "rum rows" were a regular site at the three-mile marker off American shores. Within months, massive corruption arose among law enforcement officers and public officials.

Ultimately, Prohibition resulted in *increased* consumption of alcohol, mostly in secretive, uncontrolled environments. Many who had originally supported the idea of Prohibition began asking that it be repealed. Their wish was finally granted in 1933.

What happened during Prohibition here in the United States is a good reminder of what can happen to any of us, spiritually, when we are under the curse of the law. Sin actually *increases*! The more we are told *not* to do something, the more fleshly desires seem empowered to bolt into action. The law is a breeding ground for sin.

Ten Ways to Arouse Sin

Even one of God's most devoted servants, the apostle Paul, said it was impossible for him to stop coveting when he was under the law: "But sin, seizing the opportunity afforded by the commandment, produced in me *every kind of coveting*" (Rom. 7:8).

Did you catch that? The "opportunity *afforded* by the commandment"? The law gives sin an opportunity to thrive. Not only that, but "Thou shall not covet" is the moral law. You know, the Big Ten. Paul describes this ministry "engraved in letters on stone" as a ministry that brought death and a ministry of condemnation (2 Cor. 3:7–9). "Engraved in letters on stone" means the Ten Commandments. So putting ourselves under the law, even under the Ten Commandments, results in more sinning, not less.

Why does sin naturally increase under the law? Because sinful passions are "aroused by the law" (Rom. 7:5). The bottom line is that we Christians can expect *more* struggle and *more* sinning if we are living under a set of commandments or laws. This is precisely why we're invited to live apart from law, in the radical freedom of heaven's grace. Heaven proclaims to us the counterintuitive truth that "the power of sin is the law" (1 Cor. 15:56) and "apart from the Law sin is dead" (Rom 7:8 NASB).

HEAVEN'S ALL-FRUIT DIET

The Scriptures speak clearly to God's heavenly image bearers: we are dead to the law (Rom. 7:4, 6; Gal. 2:19); we are not under law (Rom. 6:14; Gal. 5:18); we are not supervised by law (Gal. 3:25); the requirements of the law have been fully met in us (Rom. 8:3–4); the law is set aside (Eph. 2:14–15; Heb. 7:18); and Christ is the end of the law for us (Rom. 10:4).

But doesn't God ask us to keep the law with his help? Pause to consider that one for a moment. Has God placed within you an innate desire to avoid pork and shellfish or to refrain from work on Saturdays? Of course not! That's not the new covenant message. No, it's not on God's heart for us to keep the law, nor is he helping us keep it.

Instead, the fruit of God's Spirit is enough. In Galatians, we find a list of what we can expect as we trust heaven's new way—qualities like love, patience, and self-control. Then Paul says, "against such things there is no law" (Gal. 5:23). Everything we're so worried will happen if we take the law out of the picture is not *really* a concern. God's Spirit won't lead us in the direction of sin. He motivates us to live upright lives without any so-called assistance from the law. As we've seen, the law only hinders the Spirit's work in our lives (Gal. 3:1–3), causing sin to thrive. Grace does the opposite.

> Sin shall no longer be your master, *because you are not under the law*, but under grace. (Rom. 6:14)

Did you notice the *why* here? Why won't sin be our master? Because we are not under the law. Having a relationship with law invites sin into our lives. Being under God's grace is what frees us so that sin won't master us. So are you willing to invest *fully* in heaven's new way of grace?

What's the "Holdup"?

But wait. What about Romans 3:31, where Paul says we don't nullify the law but instead we "uphold the law"? If the term "uphold" here means "to obey or adhere to," this would mean that Christians should keep the law. And there's more than six hundred things to uphold! So is that what Paul means?

In context, the term "uphold" (or "establish" in the NASB) means "to hold in high regard," "to esteem," or "to establish the validity of." We should regard the law as holy, righteous, and good. But esteeming it is *not* the same as believing we are under it! Holding it in high regard is different from having to adhere to it.

It is only those who have fully embraced God's new way of grace who hold the law in highest esteem. If any person believes they should "give it their best" by trying to obey the law, they have not recognized or respected its impossible standard. They do not esteem ("uphold") the perfection of the law. They insult the law by thinking they can obey it or by merely cherry-picking portions of it to obey. This dishonors the law. We only truly respect the perfection of the law when we opt out of it entirely, recognizing our need for God's grace.

THE RULING ON RULES

But what about rules? Heaven warns us about their appeal and reveals them as a dead end:

> Why, as though you still belonged to the world, do you submit to its rules? . . . Such regulations indeed have *an appearance of wisdom* . . . but *they lack any value* in restraining sensual indulgence. (Col. 2:20, 23)

Rules are the same as law. Rules assume we are dirty and distant from God.

We didn't begin our relationship with God by rules. We began through Jesus. The Scriptures say, "So then, just as you received Christ Jesus as Lord, continue to live in him" (Col. 2:6). Similarly, Paul warns, "You foolish Galatians! . . . After beginning by means of the Spirit, are you now trying to finish by means of the flesh?" (Gal. 3:1–3).

A rule- or law-driven self-improvement program is not the way to growth. We grow just as we were saved. We grow in personal relationship with Jesus Christ. He is enough. This is heaven's next message to us.

HEAVEN SPEAKS

I have called you to a covenant of greater glory. In my faithfulness to you, I have secured for you a permanent cleanness and a permanent closeness to me. This is my new covenant promise to you. Count on it. Live from it. You have something superior, something new, something unbreakable, now and for eternity. In light of this better hope, I have set aside the old way, as it was weak and useless to you. It could never perfect you or draw you close to me.

While you were merely of this world, operating in the realm of the flesh, sin was constantly aroused in you. Lawlike demands that you called morality and ethics prodded you to do your best in human strength. But you only bore dead fruit. Now you have been released from the law that condemned you so that you can live from the desires I have placed in your heart, not from any religious "have tos." This makes all the difference, as you are motivated by me in the midst of an incredible freedom.

Do not fall victim to the old way of obligation and rules. While rules have the appearance of being effective, they have no value in restraining the lust of the eyes and the pride of the flesh. But as you walk in childlike trust with me, you walk in the victory over sin that I already purchased for you.

You were never meant to focus on avoiding sin. You are meant to fix your eyes on me. As you look to me, I enable you to overcome the pull of the world and feel the true freedom of my heavenly grace.

I love you, my dearest child.

Jesus

Awakening TO HEAVEN

Thank you, Jesus, for allowing me to participate in your amazing new covenant. Thank you for securing so much for me through your efforts at the cross and through your resurrection. Thank you for making me clean. Thank you for making me close. And thank you for making it forever so. This means I don't have to spend my life trying to live by rules to avoid sin. Instead, I can fix my eyes on you and walk by your Spirit. That's the only way I can really avoid sin. You've made it about relationship with you, not a long list of obligations. For that, I am so grateful.

I love you, Jesus, and I love your new way of grace.

Heaven Speaks inspired by 2 Corinthians 3:10–11, 17; Hebrews 7:18–19; 8:6; 12:2; Romans 6:17, 20; 7:6; Galatians 5:1, 16; Colossians 2:20–23; 1 John 2:16.

3

Here's a riddle for you: What's high and long and strung all over? It can turn dozens of square miles into a single home, and even the Capitol, the White House, and the Supreme Court have one surrounding them.

Give up? It's an *eruv*. An eruv is a wire that is strung to surround an open, public area in order to make it "private," at least in the minds of those who hope God sees it the same way!

On the Sabbath, the law prohibits orthodox Jews to carry or transport anything from one "domain" to another or from an enclosed area to an open area (Exod. 16:29). So for years, many outdoor activities in communities like Washington, DC, and Miami Beach came to a screeching halt for local Jews each Friday evening at sundown and didn't resume until twenty-four hours later.

But recently, all of that changed. Like many other Jewish communities, the Miami Beach community has implemented a work-around, a "loophole" of sorts. By stringing an eruv, a single strand of wire wrapped around thirty square miles at Miami Beach, the Jewish residents converted a very open, public area into an "enclosed" home of sorts. This imaginary boundary now enables them to do all the driving, transporting of packages, and shuttling of their children that they want on the Sabbath without that guilty feeling they might otherwise experience from violating one of the Ten Commandments—remembering the Sabbath day and keeping it holy.

Loopholes and work-arounds—this is the only way any of us can possibly claim that adhering to the law is a real possibility. Whether it's the dietary restrictions or the wardrobe regulations or, in this case, one of the Ten Commandments, we humans can't actually keep the law. We can fabricate the appearance of doing so, but living under the law inevitably yields defeat if you're honest or hypocrisy if you're not. And this comes as no shock to the God who makes us to die to the law (Gal. 2:19) so that we might *genuinely* live for him!

CONVICTS AND CORPSES

My friend Travis is a state trooper. He's had many adventures out here in West Texas. Recently, Travis helped capture a guy who was escaping down the highway after attempting to carry out some bank robberies. Travis and his fellow officers laid the road spikes that brought the guy's vehicle to a screeching halt. They arrested him and dragged him away for trial.

But imagine if, when they approached that vehicle, they had found the guy dead. Maybe he'd had a heart attack from the high-speed chase. Then would they haul him away for trial? Would he even have to pay a fine for speeding?

Of course not. We don't prosecute dead people. The law has no jurisdiction over a corpse. In the same way, we Christians have died to the law, and it has no jurisdiction over us:

> Do you not know, brothers and sisters—for I am speaking to those who know the law—that *the law has authority over someone only as long as that person lives*? . . . So, my brothers and sisters, you also *died to the law* through the body of Christ, that you might belong to another, to him who was raised from the dead, in order that we might bear fruit for God. (Rom. 7:1, 4)

God the Father is clear on the matter. We the church are the bride of his Son. We are joined to him and one spirit with him (1 Cor. 6:17). Our relationship with the law is over. Any guilt or fear is only found in an adulterous return to the law. The destiny we are called to is an incredible rest and a beautiful freedom. This can only be experienced through realizing our death to the law.

Observe the Obsolete?

The wind-up watch is now obsolete. The watch market is dominated these days by digital quartz watches with alarms, stopwatches, calendars, and lithium batteries. Many of us don't even wear a watch at all anymore. We just look to our phones.

The writer of Hebrews tells us that the old covenant is also obsolete, aging, and soon to disappear: "By calling this covenant 'new,' he has made the first one obsolete; and what is obsolete and aging will soon disappear" (Heb. 8:13). Soon disappear? So is the law still around?

Jesus said the law wouldn't go away until heaven and earth disappear (Matt. 5:18). And last time I checked, heaven and earth are still here. This means that the law still has a function today. But if Christians are dead to the law and the old covenant is now obsolete, then what function could the law have?

Paul tells us that the law isn't for Christians; it's for the unrighteous sinner alone (1 Tim. 1:8–10). As we've already seen, the law shows us our sin when we are lost. In that way, it's our tutor that leads us to Christ. But once we come to Christ, we are no longer in need of that tutor (Gal. 3:24–25).

So while the law is still around today, without the smallest letter or stroke having disappeared from it (Matt. 5:18), thank God that we Christians are *dead* to it!

THE LAW IN MY HEART?

But some sort of laws *are* written in our hearts and minds. We know this from Scripture (Heb. 10:16). But is it *Old Testament* law that is written on our hearts? That would be a return to law, wouldn't it?

The simple truth is that it's God's new *laws* (plural), not the Old Testament law, that are written on our hearts. Jesus and the apostle John both tell us what these new laws are:

> A *new* command I give you: *Love one another. As I have loved you*, so you must love one another. (John 13:34)

> And this is his command: to *believe* in the name of his Son, Jesus Christ, and to *love one another as he commanded us*. (1 John 3:23)

> In fact, this is love for God: to keep his commands. And *his commands are not burdensome*. (1 John 5:3)

Jesus was surrounded by his Jewish contemporaries who were very familiar with the commands in the Old Testament law. But Jesus announced to them, "A *new* command I give you" (John 13:34). This signals that Jesus was *not* referring to the Old Testament law of "Love your neighbor as yourself" (Lev. 19:18). Instead, he was saying, "Love each other as I have loved you" (John 15:12).

Heaven isn't sending us mixed messages about the role of the law in our lives today. We are free from the law, period. The new covenant commands written in our hearts are belief in Jesus and loving others in the same way that he has loved us. These commands will never be burdensome to us. And we can rest assured that "love covers over a multitude of sins" (1 Pet. 4:8).

Here's heaven's next message to us about this astounding freedom.

HEAVEN SPEAKS

My goal for you is love from a pure heart and a good conscience. This only happens by living from my grace. Some depart from grace early in their walk with me and try to live for me by returning to law-centered religiosity. In so doing, they miss the freedom and joy I have provided. My heartfelt cry for you is that you soak in the depths of my love for you. Let me sustain you, motivate you, animate your every move.

So just as you received me, walk in me, rooted and grounded in my grace. Do you remember what you did to receive me? You simply admitted you could not save yourself. You let me save you. In the same way, you can now wake up each day and remember that apart from my Spirit, you can do nothing.

My grace deactivates the pride of the flesh. While religious standards spur human effort to seek perfection, my Spirit prompts you to rest in me and the perfection I have already given you. As you relax in what I've done for you, you exude my fruit to those around you. This is the life I intend for you. Anything else is a performance trap.

The law is my perfect tool to show the dirt on humanity's face. It was meant for the Jews, my people under the old way. Those under my new way, like you, are destined for freedom. But if you're not careful, any form of law will hold you hostage. You're not meant to be locked up by the law. You're designed for the liberty of my grace.

The enemy invites you to abuse your liberty and continue in sin. But freedom to sin is only the illusion of freedom. Real freedom is freedom from sin. That is the freedom I purchased for you. Through my new way, you are invited to the table of grace to feast on my goodness. The weight of the law and the weight of sin need not hang around your neck. You are connected to me and me alone.

My command for you today is simple: to believe in me and to love one another even as I have loved you. So I'm giving you a greater, higher command under my new way. I'm asking you to set your mind on how much I love you, to absorb my love, and then to transmit my love to others. This command is not burdensome. Its fulfillment flows from my presence in you, as I have poured out my love in your heart through my Spirit.

I know you worry about the freedom of grace and where it might lead. You feel you need something else to guard you. But I am your Guardian, my dear child. I will never fail to give you my guidance. I will even enable you to think my very thoughts, as I have given you a new mind, my mind.

Trust me. Trust my love. I am enough.

Jesus

Awakening TO HEAVEN

When I get sidetracked in trying to work for you, to impress you, I only find myself exhausted. Thank you that these moments only bring a greater awareness of my need for you. I ask you to remind me, in the times I need it most, that your life dwells in me, that my relationship to the old way of law religion is over, and that you are enough for me. I cherish the freedom you have given me. I celebrate you and the liberty of your love. I love you, Jesus.

Heaven Speaks inspired by 1 Timothy 1:5; Galatians 3:3, 23; 5:13, 18; Titus 2:11–12; Ephesians 3:17–19; Colossians 2:6–7; John 13:34; 15:5; Romans 3:20; 5:5; 6:1–2, 7; 8:14; 9:31; Hebrews 10:14; Matthew 11:28–30; Acts 15:10; 1 John 3:23; 5:3; 1 Corinthians 2:16.

4

The bridge is closed because of protests," he said.

"Bridge? What bridge? And protests? For how long?" I asked, my voice rising.

We'd been sitting in a line of bumper-to-bumper traffic for hours. What was going on? And why were there hundreds of people on foot? I got out of the car and walked across the street to ask one of them if they knew what was happening.

My wife, our three-year-old son, and I were visiting relatives serving as Wycliffe missionaries in a remote village of Mexico. We had a relaxing vacation in mind, and we were almost at our destination. But it appeared our plans were coming to an unexpected halt as some sort of protests were going on and the protesters had barricaded the bridge, preventing traffic from crossing.

"How long do you think it will be?" I asked the man.

"Not sure, but last time it was two days before they let people through."

Two days! We had very little food and water with us, and there were no restaurants or stores in sight. We couldn't afford to spend two days in our car, especially with little Gavin with us.

We waited two more hours before traffic started to move again. The cars in front of us crept along for miles as apparently the protesters were letting cars through. But just as we got to the front of the line where we could see the bridge and the protesters, their generosity was over. They shut the bridge down again and barricaded the entrance. We were only three cars away from getting through, and now the wait had started all over again!

We couldn't sit around any longer. As we saw it, there were only two choices: (1) reason with the protesters, asking them to let our car through, or (2) abandon our car entirely and try walking across the bridge with the local foot traffic. We could see police cars and taxis on the far side of the bridge, and it looked as though the taxis were transporting people to their destinations. So we popped open the trunk, grabbed our suitcases, and abandoned our rental car (sorry, Hertz). Katharine was dragging two suitcases behind her toward the bridge and the protesters. I too had one rolling along behind me, and I was pushing Gavin in his stroller in front.

When we reached the bridge, we were greeted by an unexpected sight. The protesters were wielding machetes and holding cans of burning hot oil with open flames on top. We weren't sure what to make of it, whether we were in danger or not. So we put our heads down and kept walking, trying not to stand out in the crowd.

But while we were trying to avoid notice, little Gavin had ideas of his own. When he saw the cans of fire, he thought it was a birthday party of some sort. And when he saw the machetes, he wondered when they'd be cutting the cake! So he started yelling from his stroller. First he tried a bit of the Spanish he knew, screaming "hola" at the protesters. Then he began practicing his animal noises at full volume. No amount of shushing was having any effect.

Despite glares from the armed protesters, we eventually made it across the bridge and hopped in a taxi. And once we were safely tucked away in our beds that night, our fear became nothing more than a distant memory.

Jesus the Bridge

I share this true story of our frightening bridge crossing to make a point: crossing over to the new covenant can be just as scary! Voices around us try to hold the bridge hostage as they protest the idea of freedom. Armed with the law in hand, they tell us we have no business crossing over. They warn us that being safely tucked away in Jesus and resting in his love is nothing more than a pipe dream. And to bolster the fear, they quote the harsh teachings of Jesus at us and tell us to "get busy trying."

So how do we cross over? And how can we afford to cross over to a place of grace when the fiery teachings of Jesus are staring us in the face?

When most of us think of Jesus's life on earth, we might think of his incredibly loving teachings about our union with him, the vine and the branches, the coming Holy Spirit, and the celebration of the Lord's Supper—the "new covenant in my blood" (Luke 22:20). But there's a flip slide to Jesus's teachings, because he served as the bridge between the old way of the law and heaven's new way.

Have you ever stopped to consider that Jesus actually said things like these?

- Cut off your hand (Matt. 5:30; 18:8; Mark 9:43).
- Pluck out your eye (Matt. 5:29; 18:9; Mark 9:47).
- Beat the Pharisees at their own righteousness game (Matt. 5:20).
- Forgive others in order to be forgiven by God (Matt. 6:14–15).
- Be perfect just like God (Matt. 5:48).

- Sell everything you have (Matt. 19:21; Mark 10:21; Luke 18:22).

How would these teachings make his audience feel? Free? Absolutely not. So how do they fit with feeling the freedom of grace? After all, Jesus even went on to say things like:

> *You have heard* that it was said to the people long ago, "You shall not murder, and anyone who murders will be subject to judgment." *But I tell you* that anyone who is angry with a brother or sister will be subject to judgment. (Matt. 5:21–22)

> *You have heard* that it was said, "You shall not commit adultery." *But I tell you* that anyone who looks at a woman lustfully has already committed adultery with her in his heart. (Matt. 5:27–28)

What did Jesus mean by "you have heard that it was said"? Jesus was referring to the Old Testament law. And he was expanding on the law, raising the standard. Jesus was making it impossible for anyone to comply with his teaching. Cut off your hand? Now that's commitment in your fight against sin! Pluck out your eye? That's dedication! Oh, and by the way, sell everything in order to enter the kingdom of heaven—how many of us have done that one? And finally, in case we didn't know exactly what the standard was, "be perfect as your heavenly

Father is perfect" (Matt. 5:48). Ouch, that's gonna leave a mark!

So how did people feel when they heard this message? Many were frustrated, feeling they'd already tried their best. They were discouraged, recognizing they'd never reach their goal. They were saddened and despairing, burdened in a way they'd never even imagined, with no hope of ever freeing themselves from the crushing weight of God's true expectations for them.

Do you see the flip side of Jesus's ministry? Not only was he prophesying about a new way to come, but he was also *burying people under the old way of the law*.

Jesus Christ is the dividing line of human history. His life served as the means for two different ministries at once. He is the bridge from old to new.

This is heaven's next message for us.

HEAVEN SPEAKS

Just at the right time, I entered your world. I walked in the midst of all the hustle and bustle of downtown Jerusalem, where the priests offered their sacrifices in hopes of appeasing my Father. But this new priesthood, my priesthood, is heavenly and different. And when the priesthood changed, everything changed.

Under the old way, I could never have served as priest. Only those in the line of Levi were eligible. Father arranged for me to be born into the line of Judah, departing from the regulations of the old. This enabled my priesthood to stand out as the beginning of a whole new era.

So I am your priest, and the new way is your only covenant hope. I purchased you away from condemnation and adopted you as my own. While some misunderstood the old way and tried to make themselves holy through it, I have made you holy through the one-time sacrifice of my body. Through my new way, you are forever holy!

Since you are in me, you can see behind the veil of the law to realize that it was only given to point humanity toward me. Now that you are joined to me, the veil has been taken away, and you can see my simple, loving will for you. I want you to know me, share yourself with me, and enjoy life as a healthy, flourishing branch, bearing my fruit. I want this for you because I love you so deeply.

The law was only a dim picture of a more beautiful reality—me in you, your true hope. I have woven my desires into the lining of your heart so that you can live freely from the core of your being. You'll be surprised at just how intuitive your new life can become.

I love you, and I am life to you.

Jesus

Awakening TO HEAVEN

Thank you, Jesus, for dying to bring the new way inaugurated in your blood. You have given me a covenant of life. By this greater covenant, you have made me holy and one with you. I see that I am free from the obligation of rules as I live and walk by your Spirit in me.

I will forever honor your eternal, heavenly priesthood. Thank you for purchasing me and placing me firmly under the new way so that I may be rooted and grounded in your grace. I will celebrate you and the new way you have paved for me, without compromise. I choose to reject the guilt and fear of the old way. I choose to feel the freedom of your grace, as this is my destiny.

I love you, Jesus.

Heaven Speaks inspired by Romans 5:6; 8:15–16; Galatians 4:4–5; Hebrews 7:12–14; 9:16–17; 10:1, 10, 16; 1 Corinthians 6:11; 2 Corinthians 3:14–16; John 15:5; Colossians 2:16–17.

5

**[Jesus was] born of a woman,
born under the law.**

Galatians 4:4

We put a check mark next to "born of a woman" on our theology quiz, and we pass with flying colors. The virgin birth is a no-brainer for us Christians. But "born under the law"—huh? Many of us haven't thought much about that one. Not only was Jesus born under the law, but his audience at that time was described as "those under the law" (Gal. 4:4–5).

Flip over to Matthew 1 and then turn back one page, and you'll find the title "The New Testament" printed there. But is Matthew 1 really the beginning of the New Testament era?

Actually, no.

When did the new covenant really begin if Jesus was born under the law? Hebrews tells us that "a will is in force only when someone has *died*" (Heb. 9:17). If you try to enforce your will before your death, it's not happening. The government won't have it. You've got to be dead to enforce your will and pass on your wealth.

Why is there talk of a "will" in the book of Hebrews? Actually, it's quite clever. The words *will*, *testament*, and *covenant* are all the same word in the original language. We still use the expression "my last will and testament" today when referring to the official document. The writer of Hebrews is saying that just as someone's will doesn't go into effect without a death, so God's new covenant didn't go into effect before Jesus's death. So it was Jesus's death, not his birth, that brought in the New Testament era.

Remember that even the old covenant wasn't inaugurated without blood. Moses sprinkled blood all over the scroll and all over the people. Now, that's a church service I'd be happy to miss! Similarly, it was Jesus's blood shed on Calvary that brought in heaven's new way, changing everything.

This is important to recognize. It helps us understand the two-pronged ministry of Jesus: burying people under the true spirit of the law and simultaneously speaking of something brand-new to come. Realizing Jesus's true intent with his harsh teachings helps us feel the freedom of grace as we live on *this* side of the cross.

"Observe All That I Commanded You"

Jesus told his disciples to teach people to "observe all that I commanded you" (Matt. 28:20 NASB). So aren't Jesus's harshest teachings for us to obey?

There's no question that Jesus told his disciples to preach the gospel and to teach others what he had commanded them to teach. But here's a question: Do you believe the disciples obeyed Jesus? I certainly do. And where can we find the result of their obedience? In the epistles they wrote!

The epistles reflect what Jesus commanded them to teach. Yet nowhere do Peter, James, or John ask us to sell our possessions to enter the kingdom, as Jesus commanded in Matthew 19:21. Nor do the apostles tell us to sever body parts, if necessary, in our fight against sin, as Jesus taught in Matthew 5:29–30. Finally, they do not suggest that if we fail to take extreme measures like these, we will be "thrown into hell," as Jesus taught in Matthew 5:22 and 29–30.

These harsh teachings of Jesus are conspicuously absent from the apostles' instruction to the New Testament church. They do not appear in any epistle or in any sermons delivered by the apostles in Acts. Why not? We have two possible answers. Either the apostles deliberately disobeyed Jesus and filtered his teaching after he ascended, or—and this is more likely—those harsh teachings are *not* what Jesus commanded the apostles to teach!

Jesus knew full well how much life would change under the new covenant initiated by his blood. And the teaching that Jesus intended us to receive through the apostles was the new covenant teaching of grace. That's what we find in the epistles, which are the *result* of the apostles' obedience to Jesus.

Trying to Be "Great" for God

In Matthew 5, Jesus says that whoever practices his harsh teachings will be "called great" in the kingdom. What does that mean? Here's how Jesus puts it:

> Anyone who sets aside one of the least of these commands and teaches others accordingly will be called least in the kingdom of heaven, but *whoever practices and teaches these commands will be called great* in the kingdom of heaven. (Matt. 5:19)

At first glance, it seems as if Jesus expects us to keep his harsh teachings to become "great" in heaven. And we might even think the same after reading Paul's statement about law abiders:

> For it is not those who hear the law who are righteous in God's sight, but it is *those who obey the law who will be declared righteous.* (Rom. 2:13)

This seems to suggest there are people who can truly practice these commands, some who can be labeled "doers" of the law. As Romans continues, however, we discover the exact number of people who have successfully practiced the law and, by extension, the number of people who will be called "great" in heaven:

> Now we know that whatever the law says, it says to those who are under the law, so that *every mouth may be silenced* and the whole world held accountable to God. Therefore *no one will be declared righteous in God's sight by the works of the law*; rather, through the law we become conscious of sin. (Rom. 3:19–20)

So how many human beings have successfully practiced the law? Zero. And in the Gospels, Jesus is quoting the law and raising the standard. He's making it even more difficult to follow the law. If no one could keep the original law, how many will succeed under the more challenging version of the law that Jesus introduced? The answer, again, is zero. Through the law we encounter failure, not success.

Jesus puts an end to any hopes and dreams of being great in heaven: "For I tell you that unless your righteousness *surpasses that of the Pharisees and the teachers of the law*, you will certainly not enter the kingdom of heaven" (Matt. 5:20). According to Jesus's performance demands, we have to do better than all of the Pharisees and scribes *just to enter* heaven, much less be great when we get there. Upon hearing that last bit, his listeners' hearts sank, I'm sure.

Jesus wasn't naïve when he presented them with this unattainable standard. He knew full well they couldn't even approach the level of righteousness he introduced. As Galatians 4:4–5 reveals, Jesus was born under the law, and the goal of his teaching was to redeem those under the law. How would he redeem them? The first step was to make them realize that any attempts of their own to "be perfect" were futile.

Heaven has announced a covenant to us that was inaugurated in Jesus's blood. It was Jesus's death at Calvary (not his birth in Bethlehem!) that initiated the New Testament era. This truth illuminates the purpose behind the harsh teachings of Jesus. And it enables us to feel the *pure* freedom of God's grace, here on this side of the cross.

Here's heaven's next message to us.

HEAVEN SPEAKS

I was born under the law in order to fully meet its requirements so that you wouldn't have to. Through my death, heaven ushered in a new way for you, and Father's ancient promise to Abraham was kept.

Although some look to my birth as the beginning of the new way, it was my death that started it all. Just as an inheritance requires the death of the one who left it, my death brought you an inheritance beyond your wildest imagination.

I have had many faithful servants throughout history. But through my new way, I have given you something better than any servant of old ever experienced. Yes, those who came before you expressed incredible faith in me, to the point of suffering, even dying, for my name.

Still, I saved my very best for you.

Consider your favorite hero from the Old Testament. I have made your relationship with me better than anything they could ever enjoy! Because you live on this side of my death and look back on my finished work, you benefit in a way that even David, a man after my own heart, could not.

The ministry of the law came on the scene with a certain glory. When Moses came down from the mountain, my people could not look him in the face because of the glow of its glory. Despite the glory of the law, it still only brought condemnation and death to everyone. But my blood inaugurated a new and living way of much greater glory. Compared to the surpassing glory of my new way, the law now has no glory at all.

So there is no reason to flirt with the old way. You cannot mix death with life. The covenant you participate in is one of life, my life. I've called you out to celebrate the freedom of this new life with me.

Jesus

Awakening TO HEAVEN

Jesus, you revealed the true spirit of the law to all those around you. Life with you in your kingdom cannot be earned; no amount of effort could possibly attain it. Thank you, Jesus, that it's all about you and your efforts on my behalf. Thank you for your promise to be my High Priest forever, no matter what. I put full confidence in the truth of your new covenant promises. Thank you for forgiving me, cleansing me, and making me right. Thank you for placing your resurrection life in me and equipping me to minister your new way to others.

I love you, Jesus.

Heaven Speaks inspired by Galatians 3:16–29; 4:4–5; Romans 8:3–4; Hebrews 9:16–17; 11:39–40; 2 Corinthians 3:7–11.

6

The movie *The Shawshank Redemption* paints a vivid picture of how inmates who've been incarcerated for decades struggle to cope with freedom once their sentence is over. First, an elderly man named Brooks is released. He finds himself without direction and, seemingly, without hope. Eventually, Brooks can't handle the life of freedom. He commits suicide, hanging himself in his apartment. He'd rather be dead than wrestle with the unnerving freedom of life outside of prison.

Another prisoner named Red is also released from prison. As fate would have it, he ends up in the same apartment that Brooks once rented. Red even discovers the spot where Brooks hung himself along with the note "Brooks was here" etched in a wood beam.

But things turn out differently for Red. He decides to take full advantage of his freedom. While he's tempted to commit some silly crime just to return to the confines of prison, he finally decides to embrace his freedom. He travels south to Zihuatanejo, Mexico, where he joins his friend Andy in a sunny paradise.

THE RISK OF FREEDOM

Freedom. There are many different reactions to the idea. Some feel so secure within the bounds of the law that freedom is just too intimidating. Others put one foot in freedom while keeping the other foot firmly rooted in the law. You know, just in case.

It's difficult to allow ourselves to enjoy freedom. Like Red, we may even find ourselves tempted to commit a silly sin just to see how free we really are and what God is going to "do about it." Then we expect that we'll need the law again to pull ourselves up by our bootstraps. But God won't have it. He intends for our attitudes and actions to be motivated by freedom, from start to finish.

Freedom feels risky. And freedom means personal responsibility. Freedom means we can't pull out a measuring stick to evaluate our status. It means we are accepted, no matter what. It also means that our life choices will have to be motivated by something other than guilt or fear. New covenant freedom releases us to allow God's Spirit to be all that he desires to be in our lives: "where the Spirit of the Lord is, there is liberty" (2 Cor. 3:17 NASB).

When we Christians argue for the law in our lives, it's like fashioning a safety net for our behavior. But heaven is calling us to cut through the safety net of the law and walk the tightrope of grace. When we do, we find ourselves mysteriously balanced by Christ within. We're designed to trust Jesus, not only for our final destination but also for our character along the way.

Owing God

The bottom line of this freedom is that we don't owe God anything! But this is hard for us to believe. Growing up in Christian homes, schools, or churches, we might hear, "Jesus has done so much for you. What will you do for him in return?" Then we set out to make sacrifices to "pay him back" for everything he has done for us. But the certificate of debt has been canceled and taken out of the way (Col. 2:14).

What if the "sacrifice" that heaven wants is for us to awaken our senses to the wonders of God's grace and simply give thanks?

> Through Him then, let us continually offer up a *sacrifice of praise* to God, that is, *the fruit of lips that give thanks* to His name. (Heb. 13:15 NASB)

A true sacrifice is the fruit of lips that give thanks to God. That's what heaven wants—a thankful heart.

Imagine a friend shows up on your doorstop with a birthday gift for you, a gift you didn't expect. As you thank your friend and wave good-bye, you watch him get back in the car and drive away. Then you open the gift. It's nice. Ooh, it looks expensive. Then what? The guilt sets in. When was your friend's last birthday? And did you get him anything?

It's really hard for us to just *receive*. We feel as if we should give in return, and when we can't or haven't, we're flooded with guilt. We try to pay people back in some way—through gifts, or favors, or friendship. Leaving it at a heartfelt "thank you" and cherishing the gift just feels, well, selfish.

But the idea that we could pay God back, especially for what he has done for us through the death and resurrection of Jesus, is nothing short of absurd. Heaven and earth are his, and he owns the cattle on a thousand hills (Ps. 50:10). He has made everything and needs nothing from us. He is not served by our human hands as if he needed anything (Acts 17:25). Instead, he gives life and breath to all things.

Who has ever given God a gift that he didn't already own? So instead of trying to give to God, how about receiving from him? Our God calls us to receive freely from his Spirit. There's no other way to awaken to the freedom of grace. It's all about receiving and walking in thankfulness. And that's heaven's next message to us.

HEAVEN SPEAKS

Not only does my grace save you and hold you tight for eternity, but it also molds you and shapes you so that you draw life from me. The self-control you so desperately seek is found in the character of my Spirit. It is my fruit, not your own, and I am released in your life through the power of my grace. The result is always a godly life, because I am God, and I am your life. There is no other form of godliness outside of me.

I will work mightily in you to live a life that you cannot otherwise live. It is you and me in union that results in a life motivated by grace. My grace is not just forgiveness and a new destination; by grace I have given you my life. I have given you a place of honor, right next to me. From this heavenly vantage point, you live life and can choose wisely from the options on earth. Regardless of your choices, I will never revoke your calling or the gifts I have given you. I accept you and embrace you, with no strings attached!

Still, if you use your freedom to indulge the flesh, you will surely be disappointed. I have designed you to be most fulfilled when your life is an expression of me. And as my life overflows through yours, you sow seeds in the lives of people you love.

No matter what you do in this life, do it with thankfulness to me. It's not that I need the thanks. But setting your mind on all that I am to you liberates you to live in gratefulness, a powerful motivator in your life. You will give and live cheerfully from the heart, not from pressure. I jealously want that for you. I love you, and I so long for you to freely enjoy all the grace I have lavished on you.

Jesus

Awakening TO HEAVEN

Jesus, thank you for the freedom of your grace. Thank you for holding me in your arms and never letting me go. I trust you for heaven. But even more, I trust you for my daily living. Your Spirit is the source of all goodness produced in me. I do not fully understand how the freedom you have given me frees me from sin's power, but you say it is so. You say that apart from the law, sin is dead. I believe you and ask you to awaken my senses to the wonders of your grace. I love you and cannot thank you enough for honoring me with freedom.

Heaven Speaks inspired by Titus 2:11–12; 2 Corinthians 3:17; 9:7; Galatians 5:13, 22–23; Colossians 1:29; 3:1–4, 17; Romans 6:5; 11:29; 1 Corinthians 6:17; John 10:10; Ephesians 1:6; 2:6; Philippians 2:3–4; 1 Thessalonians 5:11, 18.

HEAR
THE SPIRIT
BEARING WITNESS

The Spirit himself bears
witness with our spirit that
we are children of God.

Romans 8:16 ESV

7

Identity theft is a form of fraud in which someone uses your personal information and leaves you with some damaging and costly consequences. It used to be that a thief rummaged through the dumpster behind your house to find your credit card receipts. But today, hackers steal your personal data right off your computer, your mobile phone, or even the servers where you work. According to Carnegie Mellon University, the probability of becoming a victim to identity theft due to a data breach is about 2 percent. But that number is on the rise as new computer software is making it easier and easier for even amateur hackers to succeed.

While identity theft has become a more visible problem in recent decades, its roots go all the way back to the Garden of Eden. It was there that Adam lost his spiritual identity due to a stealthy deceiver, and by extension we too lost our identity.

Born in God's Image?

Because of Adam's sin, we show up on planet earth spiritually dead, devoid of God's life (Rom. 5:15, 18). Although it's common to hear that we're all born in God's image, the Scriptures reveal that we are actually born *in Adam's image.*

> When God created mankind, he made them in the likeness of God. He created them male and female and blessed them. And he named them "Mankind" when they were created. When Adam had lived 130 years, he had a son *in his own likeness, in his own image.* (Gen. 5:1–3)

While Adam was originally created in God's image, Satan managed to steal that identity from him, and from us. The fall changed everything. As a result of the fall in Eden, we are born in Adam's spiritual image, not God's image. It is only when we receive new life in our spirits that we are re-created and renewed again in God's image. We regain the spiritual identity that God intended for us:

> Do not lie to each other, since you have taken off your old self with its practices and have put on the new self, which is *being renewed in knowledge in the image of its Creator.* (Col. 3:9–10)

Thanks to our death with Jesus, we're now re-born. We're plugged in to the life of God. We've been re-created in the image of Jesus Christ (1 John 4:17). As new creations, we are *already* like Christ in our human spirits. And we are called to live out this new identity as our minds get renewed to the truth of who we really are at the core.

All of this brings real meaning to the idea of being "born again." We need a fresh start. There's no cleaning up of the old. It can only be replaced. This is precisely what happens to us at salvation—the old goes away and the new arrives (2 Cor. 5:17). We are reborn in God's spiritual image.

SAFE AT LAST!

This news is incredibly comforting. Because we are now in Christ, we are in a safe place. We are "hidden with Christ in God" (Col. 3:3).

Have you thought about what it means to be enveloped along with Christ inside of God himself? We toss around phrases like "being out of fellowship" and "trying to get close to God." All the while, God's Spirit is bearing witness, if we would only listen, that we are *one spirit with him* (1 Cor. 6:17). We are hidden safely in him right next to Jesus.

Can you get any closer than that? We are in the safest of spiritual locations, being hugged tight by the King himself. We are as safe as his only begotten

Son (1 John 4:17), because he has purchased us and bestowed on us his own righteousness and holiness:

> It is because of him that you are in Christ Jesus, who has become for us wisdom from God—that is, our righteousness, holiness and redemption. (1 Cor. 1:30)

Many of us are quick to say that we are redeemed, as the verse above indicates. But we are slow to agree that we are also righteous and holy. "Oh, yeah, in Christ" we say, as if that's some sort of distant, far-off righteousness that is useless for now. But how righteous are you if Christ Jesus has become your righteousness? And how holy are you if Christ Jesus has become your holiness? These are qualities that we possess because Jesus has become our life (Col. 3:4).

Once we realize our crucifixion, burial, and resurrection with Jesus Christ, we can see that God announces us as righteous and holy because he is describing our nature. He does more than put a righteous label on us. He does more than merely adopt us into his family. In our human spirits, *he has made us like him* (1 John 4:17).

Heaven Ready!

We are righteous. We are holy. God sees us this way because we *are* this way!

Think about it—where do the Scriptures speak of a future polish that we get right before we hit heaven? Nowhere! Yes, we get a new body when we escape this world, but not a new human spirit or soul. Why not? Because our "inner man" is heaven ready, right here and now. In our human spirit, we are already seated in heaven (Eph. 2:6).

The two realms coexist—the physical and the spiritual. One is no less real than the other. In fact, the spiritual has permanence, while the physical will one day fade away and be replaced. Everything that we see and touch will be destroyed and replaced, but our human spirits will live forever. The spiritual is the lasting reality.

So God invites us to recognize an invisible yet enduring reality—that we are new, that we are one with him, and that we are seated with him in heaven already. Can you hear the Spirit bearing witness?

Here's heaven's next message to us.

HEAVEN SPEAKS

I have taken every measure as the careful overseer of your soul. I bore your sins in my body on the cross. And through my wounds, you've been healed of the spiritual sickness you once knew. In my wisdom, I forgave you and lavished you with my liberating grace.

Consequently, you no longer live for yourself but for me. You are now my new creation, and your old self is dead and gone. You have put on the new self. Yes, you're still being renewed in a true knowledge of me, but you can't be any newer at the core.

It's most fitting for you to set your mind on things above, where you've been raised and seated with me. You're free to choose, but don't use your freedom as an opportunity for foolish living. The outcome of those choices is only shame and disappointment. They're an expression of death. You, on the other hand, are designed to express my divine life.

You have died, and your new life is hidden safely with me. I have equipped you with everything you need for life and godliness. In my kindness, I allowed you to share in my heavenly image. Since you are born of me, my nature resides in you. You can't continue in sinful patterns without experiencing an internal resistance to it all. It simply doesn't agree with who you are now.

I am the Lord Jesus Christ, the last Adam and the life-giving Spirit. I have forgiven you and made you alive in me. Hear my Spirit bearing witness to your true identity.

Jesus

Awakening TO HEAVEN

Thank you for the second half of the gospel—that you not only forgave me but also made me new at the core. Thank you for allowing me to participate in your death, burial, and resurrection so that I might truly live. Thank you for freedom from sin's power, the freedom to say no to its allure. Remind me to set my mind on the truth of my newness in you. I cannot thank you enough for remaining with me and in me, no matter what. You could not have demonstrated your love in any greater way. You have given me a heavenly life and a heavenly hope right here and now.

I love you, Jesus.

Heaven Speaks inspired by 1 Peter 2:24–25; 4:2; Ephesians 1:8; 2:4–5; 5:3; Colossians 2:13; 3:2–4, 9–10; 2 Corinthians 5:17; Romans 6:6, 21; 8:16; John 17:23; Galatians 5:13, 17; 2 Peter 1:3–4; 1 Corinthians 15:45, 49.

8

My wife loves to read historical fiction. One of her favorite mysteries, *A Flaw in the Blood*, suggests that Queen Victoria was not deserving of her crown. In the novel, an early researcher in genetics discovers that while Victoria was a carrier of the hemophilia gene, neither her mother's nor her supposed father's family had a history of the disease! The researcher then deduces that someone else, a carrier of the hemophilia gene, must have been Victoria's real father. Queen Victoria is guilty of an elaborate cover-up to preserve her throne.

When we show up on planet earth, we too experience a "flaw in the blood." Our spiritual bloodline leaves us riddled with the disease of sin. We are "in Adam," our spiritual forefather. Our spiritual heritage comes from him. Just as we inherit physical characteristics from our parents, we inherited spiritual characteristics from our spiritual ancestor, Adam.

The only cure is to die spiritually, so we can be born again into an entirely new spiritual family. Anything less than that is what Jesus would call whitewashing a tomb—or what we might call putting Christian lipstick on a pig. But just like the alleged Queen Victoria scandal, the world is involved in an elaborate cover-up to disguise its true condition.

CHRISTIAN LIPSTICK?

Christianity at its core is *not* about behavior modification. It's not a behavior improvement program centered on a historical teacher who models goodness. No, real Christianity is about regaining what was lost in Eden—life.

We can pretty ourselves up, polish ourselves, and engage in behavior modification. Still, we are spiritually dead. We can start reading the Bible, going to church, and acting loving toward those around us. Still, we are spiritually dead. We arrive on planet earth at age zero with a set of spiritual genetics. We arrive with Adam's spiritually dead genes.

Everyone is somewhere spiritually. When we are born, we arrive in a spiritual location—we are in Adam. So if God is going to fix our problem, he

has to *change our location*. And that is precisely
what he does:

> For as *in Adam* all die, so *in Christ* all will be made
> alive. (1 Cor. 15:22)

> But by His doing you are *in Christ Jesus*, who be-
> came to us wisdom from God, and righteousness
> and sanctification, and redemption. (1 Cor. 1:30
> NASB)

> *He has delivered us* from the domain of dark-
> ness and *transferred us* to the kingdom of his be-
> loved Son. (Col. 1:13 ESV)

THE "IN" VERSES

I used to read right past verses like these that talked
about being "in" Christ. I took them to be some
sort of symbolic biblical terminology. But passages
like these describe the spiritual surgery that God
performed on us in giving us life.

It is by God's doing that we are in Christ. He is
the one who transfers us from one realm to another
kingdom entirely. He lowers the crane hook, attaches
it to us, and pulls us *out of* Adam. Then he swings
us across a great chasm and places us *in* Christ.

As we are placed in Christ, we obtain not only
a new future but also a new spiritual past. At one

time, we had Adam's past. We died because he died. We were condemned because he was condemned. But when we become new creations in Jesus Christ, we get a new past—Jesus's past. We are crucified with Christ. We are buried with Christ. And we are raised with Christ.

We are no longer the sum total of our past. Instead, we receive a new spiritual past no longer marked by our sins but rather marked by a radical surgery that took place within us. We had Adam's DNA extracted from us and replaced with Christ's DNA. We inherit Christ's spiritual characteristics. Yes, right here and right now, we are like Christ in our human spirits:

> By this, love is perfected with us, so that we may have confidence in the day of judgment; because *as He is, so also are we in this world*. (1 John 4:17 NASB)

We don't do anything to make ourselves new. Instead, something is done to us. An outside force—God himself—acts on us and changes us in a way that only he can. In fact, the idea of "change" is not adequate here. God goes further as he *exchanges* us. In place of our old self, he makes us into a new self. This new self is not some "thing" we possess. It is us! We are literally and actually new at the center of our being.

Notice that John says we are like Jesus. We are as he is. "Well, sure, when we get to heaven," we might think. No, read carefully. It says, "In this world." This means now. We have become partakers of his divine nature (2 Pet. 1:4), and we are his very righteousness (2 Cor. 5:21) right here and now.

RIGHTEOUS BY BIRTH

We don't often use the word *righteous* in everyday conversation—except maybe as slang, as in, "He is one righteous dude." But righteousness, in simple terms, means okayness. We are 100 percent okay with God because of our new birth, not because of what we do.

As we get this issue of righteousness settled in our minds, we can stop chasing after okayness. We can rest. This is what it means to *hear the Spirit bearing witness to our true identity*. He convicts us of our righteousness so we no longer hunger and thirst for more.

We see that we already have it all. What's done is done. We are okay, and we are okay forever. We have become the righteousness of God: "He made Him who knew no sin to be sin on our behalf, *so that we might become the righteousness of God in Him*" (2 Cor. 5:21 NASB).

Two Ways to Walk

At birth, we are in the flesh. The flesh-life is all we know, and it's all we can know. We begin the journey of trying to cope and live life apart from the Source of true life. We end up with all kinds of strategies for living, all kinds of coping mechanisms to gain purpose and identity.

We need purpose and identity, so apart from Christ we seek them out. We seek knowledge for the mind, fulfilling experiences for the emotions, and strength for the will. But all of these, regardless of how much "success" we have with them, are nothing more than a fabrication of God's true life. But before we are inhabited by God's Spirit, walking after the flesh is all we can do. After all, we are *in* the flesh. It's the realm from which we live.

Once we are saved, we are *in* the Spirit all the time. Our location in the Spirit is permanent. However, there are still two ways we can *walk*: we can walk according to the flesh or according to the Spirit. In each moment, we choose as an act of our will to walk one way or another. Are we being led by God's Spirit, allowing him to bear witness to our true identity and desires? Or are we heeding the call of the flesh and trying to get our needs met through other strategies?

However we choose to walk in a given moment, it's important to know we are still *in* God's Spirit. When we walk according to the flesh, we are simply not acting like who we are. Nor are we acting like who we are *in*. The source of the sinful behavior is not really us but *an outside entity* we allow to function as a parasite:

- Do not let *sin* reign that you obey *its lusts* (Rom. 6:12).
- It is *no longer I* who do it *but sin* living in me (Rom. 7:17, 20).
- I see *another* law at work in the members of my body (Rom. 7:23).

FIGHT THE RIGHT FIGHT!

In the movie *Braveheart*, a young Scotsman named Robert the Bruce is torn between the self-preserving views of the Scottish nobility and those of William Wallace, the main character. Wallace gallantly leads a rebellion, fighting for uncompromised freedom from England.

Robert eventually feels regret over his foolish decision to side with the nobility and betray Wallace. He turns to his father and says, "I don't want to lose heart. I want to believe as [Wallace] does. I will never be on the wrong side again!" Realizing he failed to take a stand with the right side, Robert then fights wholeheartedly alongside Wallace's men and helps Scotland win its freedom.

The internal struggle that Robert the Bruce experienced reminds me of what it's like to be a Christian but not know what side you're really on. In order to fight gallantly on the right side, we Christians need a couple of tough questions answered: If I'm so much like Jesus now, why do I still struggle with temptation all the time? Aren't I sort of half new and half old? These are important questions that deserve solid answers. And thankfully, there *are* solid answers that equip us to fight the good fight, confident that we are on the right team.

It is essential that we recognize the power of sin as an outside agent. It resides outside of our "inner man" in the members of our *body*. It's a parasite that can control our life—if we let it. If we let it, we end up acting on "its lusts" (Rom. 6:12), not on our own desires. If we follow the lusts of sin, then we allow a rogue force to infiltrate and deny us the privilege of transmitting God's life.

We were re-created in Christ Jesus to say no to sin and yes to who we really are. As we have our senses awakened to heaven's grace, we hear the Spirit bearing witness: We are new. We are righteous. We are *in* Christ. And we are on the right team. This is heaven's next message to us.

HEAVEN SPEAKS

Beware! There is a parasite called sin at work in your life. Even though you are a new creation, evil is right there with you. I died to sin's power, once for all, and took you with me through that death. Therefore consider yourself dead to sin and alive to me. Don't let sin reign in your body. Don't obey its lusts. Instead, offer yourself to me and offer your body as my instrument. As you do, you will experience the true fulfillment I desire for you.

Don't be deceived by the allure of sin. Sin's power seeks to dominate you, to master you. But you are designed to be controlled by my love. You'll find nothing beneficial built into your life if you succumb to the call of sin. Instead, sin's nasty network of thoughts will wreak havoc on your mind and emotions such that you'll feel you've lost your way. Sin breeds confusion, and the earthly consequences are often beyond any expectation.

I want clarity for you. I want you to see my truth and experience the benefits of all that I have invited you to. I have called you out of sin's domain into a place of light where you can see that my face is toward you.

I have handcrafted you to love those around you and think of their good. Since you live by my Spirit, keep in step with me. The fruit of my Spirit is love, joy, peace, patience, kindness, goodness, faithfulness, gentleness, and self-control. This is your destiny—to express me and bear my fruit. Abandon the empty pursuits of sin and look deeply into my Word to discover the ways I've planned for you. Seek my truth and crave it as it quenches your inborn thirst for conformity to me.

I love you. In my love, I have made you like me, equipping you with everything you'll ever need. Discover who you are and live free!

Jesus

Awakening TO HEAVEN

Thank you, Jesus, for making me new. You gave me a new heart and a new spirit, and you placed your Spirit within me. I am so grateful to belong to you and to be aligned with you. Thank you for making me family. Thank you for showing me how to rest in the righteousness you gave me. I choose to own it and rely on it so that I walk with you in unshakable confidence. I choose to believe that sinful thoughts are not of me but instead war against me. I am now obedient from the heart. Thank you for bearing witness to my radical new identity as a child of the living

God, literally and actually born as offspring
of your Spirit.
   I love you, Jesus.

Heaven Speaks inspired by Romans 6:10–13, 21; 7:17–23; 8:29; Genesis 4:7; 2 Corinthians 5:14; 1 Corinthians 6:12; 10:23; John 4:14; 15:5–8; 17:17; 1 Peter 2:9; Hebrews 13:5; Philippians 2:4; Galatians 5:22–25; 6:15–16; 1 John 4:17; 1 Corinthians 15:49; 2 Peter 1:3–4; James 1:23–24.

9

In the film *A Beautiful Mind*, the main character suffers from a schizophrenia that results in delusions of various kinds. Throughout the film, you watch him wrestling with fantasies and apparitions. He begins thinking people are after him. He starts imagining a Department of Defense contact helping him with his mission to unravel a conspiracy. All of these hallucinations seem very real to him on an experiential level. His thoughts and emotions tell him no different.

Eventually he comes to grips with the fact that he is suffering from delusions. For the rest of the movie, you watch him trying to move on with everyday life, all the while trying to ignore some very strong pulls toward fantasy. People appear to him, thoughts are presented to him, and the one and only solution is to ignore them all. As he turns a deaf ear to them and sets his mind on what is really and actually true, he experiences peace, but the temptation to revert to the old ways of delusion is still very strong!

It's not much different for us Christians. For us, what we experience mentally and emotionally in our *souls* from day to day can be very different from what we're called to set our minds on concerning our human *spirits*.

SOUL VERSUS SPIRIT

The Bible tells us that each of us is made up of three parts: a human spirit, a human soul, and a human body (1 Thess. 5:23). Understanding the difference between soul and spirit can be very helpful (Heb. 4:12).

The soul (Greek: *psyche*) is our psychology: our mind, will, and emotions. It's where we think, feel, and experience relationship with other people. In our soul, we experience wild fluctuations of thought and emotion as we go from the heights of ecstasy to the depths of despair within moments. Our feelings follow our thoughts, and our thoughts are sometimes all over the place.

Our soul is like a mirror that can reflect anything at any given time. Our soul doesn't give us our spiritual nature. Instead, it merely reflects the nature of something else in a given moment. This is why we can walk either according to the Spirit (reflecting

Christ) or according to the flesh (reflecting sin) in any moment. These occur as we set our mind one way or the other, "angling" the soul mirror.

In contrast, our spirit (Greek: *pneuma*) is a deeper place within us. Our spirit is how we relate to the spiritual realm. And our spirit is what determines our spiritual nature as humans. When we are born, we are dead to God and alive to sin in our spirit. At salvation, we become alive to God and dead to sin. We are made partakers of God's divine nature (2 Pet. 1:4) in our spirit. Our human spirit is made right with God (Rom. 5:1, 9) and sealed by the Holy Spirit forever (Eph. 1:13–14).

When we are reborn in Christ, our soul is *not* replaced or instantly reprogrammed. The psychology of our soul (mind, will, emotions) remains. In our soul, what we reflect to those around us is progressively changing by the renewing of our minds (Rom. 12:2).

In the snapshot shown here, you can see that we have the Holy Spirit residing in our human *spirit*. The nature of our spirit is now in agreement with his Spirit. We are "one spirit with Him" (1 Cor. 6:17 NASB). Note that our *soul* (psychology) is located just outside of our spirit. Remember that the soul is like a reflector and has no nature in itself. The soul can reflect anything from one moment to the next—either Spirit-motivated attitudes or thoughts from the power of sin.

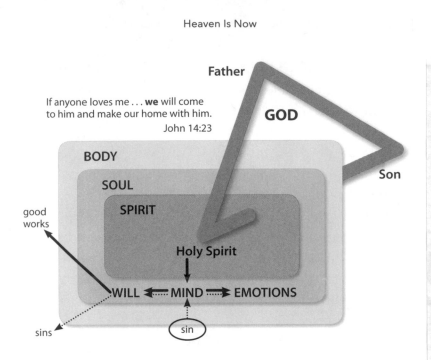

As new creations, we are designed to live from the core of our being (our human spirit), where the Holy Spirit dwells. If we choose to set our minds on the truth of our new identity, Christ is expressed and the result is good works. If we allow our soul to reflect the parasite called sin that resides in our body (Rom. 6:12; 7:23), we are acting like someone we are not: "It is no longer I who do it, but it is sin living in me" (Rom. 7:20). As our minds get renewed over time, we exchange fleshly (worldly) thinking for the heavenly "things above" (Col. 3:2).

DISCERNING THE DIFFERENCE

Discerning the difference between spirit and soul is helpful in understanding our identity in Christ. How can I be a new creation and have Christ living in me and yet still be struggling with sinful thoughts? The answer is that we are describing our *soul's experience* with temptation, not our *spirit's perfection* in Christ. Conversely, when we read the Bible and see that we have become the righteousness of God (2 Cor. 5:21) and that we have been made perfect forever (Heb. 10:14) and that we are now seated in heaven (Eph. 2:6), we wonder, "How can these verses be true of me? If you knew what my thoughts and emotions are like some days, you'd wonder if I'm even saved!" We fail to realize that heaven is describing the condition of our spirit, not the fluctuating experiences of our soul.

So discerning the difference between spirit and soul allows us to take heaven's message about our new identity at face value without watering it down. It also enables us to explain how we're still growing yet still 100 percent righteous along the way. We don't get our righteous nature from the soul. So whether our soul is reflecting the flesh or the Spirit in a given moment doesn't change the fact that we are right with God all the time in our spirit.

Of course, we will only be fulfilled as we walk according to God's Spirit. If we walk according to the flesh, we hear God's Spirit bearing witness to our true identity. God's Spirit is in agreement with our own human spirit and longs to be expressed (1 Thess. 5:19).

THEOLOGY OF THE SOUL

Now that we have distinguished soul from spirit just as the Scriptures do (1 Thess. 5:23; Heb. 4:12), we can more easily recognize what I call today's "theology of the *soul*."

Legalism is born as a theology of the soul. We feel distant in our soul. We feel dirty in our soul. And we construct theology from these feelings. All the while, God calls us to worship him "in *spirit* and truth" (John 4:24 NASB). We are not designed to let the fluctuations of the soul determine our beliefs.

On one hand, we rightly say that God will never leave us or forsake us. But then we turn around and say that we can be "out of fellowship" with God. In claiming things like these, we are describing how we *feel* in the soul.

There's no question that, when we choose sin, we are not expressing Christ. But (and this is an important *but*) even when we sin, he is still within us, living at the core of our being—in our *spirit*. The Spirit of Christ does not come and go, no matter what our soul might feel from one moment to the next. So instead of developing an "in-and-out" theology based on the roller coaster of the soul, we should be looking to the Word itself for answers. And there we find no mention of "fellowship" as something that Christians go in and out of as they behave rightly or sinfully. The Scriptures tell us that when we sin, God's Spirit is not being expressed (1 Thess. 5:19) and we may even experience painful outcomes (Rom. 6:21; Gal. 6:8) from our foolish choices. But our *spiritual* fellowship is solid and secure, unmoved by the fluctuations in our soul.

The gospel presents us with *spiritual* truths from heaven. One of these truths is that we have been dramatically changed in our human spirit. Even more, our old self has been exchanged for a new self. Rather than developing a theology of the soul, we need to understand God's theology of the *spirit*.

Yes, God created us to have a soul. And yes, we are designed to think and feel, and we should not ignore our emotions. But we shouldn't look to our soul to find truth! We don't walk by sight or by emotion. Those who worship God must worship him "in *spirit* and truth" (John 4:24 NASB). That's heaven's next message to us.

HEAVEN SPEAKS

Although you experience the ups and downs of life in your mind and emotions, I have given you everything you need within your human spirit. I have filled you with my Spirit and equipped you in every way. I removed your heart of stone and gave you a new heart like mine. This is what matters most—that you are a new creation. If you are walking in this reality, then you will find peace.

Just as I spoke the world into existence, I spoke your new spiritual heart into being. You are new at the core because of the words I have spoken to you. I took away your old self, nailing it to the cross. Then I buried your old self along with me. And just as I was raised from the dead on the third day, I raised you along with me to a newness of life.

The surgery my Spirit performed on your heart is inward, hidden. Your praise is from me, not those around you. I have placed my desires on your mind and heart so that you know what they are and desire them yourself. You are aligned with me, and we agree.

There are times you're confused about what you want. You experience the chaos of the world, and you start to wonder. But even in those times, you can know that you and I are one. We want the same thing, as we share in the same life.

As you wake up every day and live in the midst of everything earthly, remember that you, at your spiritual core, are heavenly. You are a member of a royal priesthood on earth, an alien and a stranger in the world. You are my handiwork, without blemish and free from accusation. I love all that I have made you to be.

My Word is meant as a mirror into your spirit. It is designed as the most perfect reminder of who you are. If you find yourself not being a "doer" of my Word, it's only because you've walked away from the mirror and forgotten who you are. The best cure is to gaze long and deep into the mirror of my Word and gather in all that I have said about who you really are.

I love you.

Jesus

Awakening TO HEAVEN

Thank you, Jesus, for equipping me and making me complete in you. I often find myself doubting and wondering if I need more of you to be made whole. I realize now that these are the fluctuations of my soul, in my mind and emotions. Even when the storms of the soul rage, my spirit is still firmly anchored to yours. We are one, and I cannot thank you enough for meeting my deepest need in this life and beyond.

Teach me to turn a deaf ear to the sales pitch of the enemy that says I need more. Teach me to rest in you. I choose to offer my body to you, recognizing that I am dead to sin and alive to you. I feel privileged to be included in the honor of reflecting your Spirit. I love you, Jesus.

Heaven Speaks inspired by 2 Peter 1:3–4, 8–9; Romans 2:29; 5:5; 6:4–6, 17; Galatians 2:20; 4:6; 6:15–16; Ezekiel 36:26; John 15:3; Colossians 1:22; 2:11–13; 3:4; Hebrews 8:10; 10:16; Philippians 2:13; 1 Corinthians 6:17; 1 Peter 2:9–11; Ephesians 5:26–27; James 1:23–24.

SEE
THE FINISHED
WORK OF JESUS

When he had received the
drink, Jesus said, "It is
finished." With that, he bowed
his head and gave up his spirit.

John 19:30

10

Near the end of the nineteenth century in West Africa, a currency called "Kissi money" emerged. Blacksmiths hand made this currency by twisting iron into foot-long bars. These iron bars had a sharpened *I* shape on one end and a spatula-like shape on the other. Large amounts of Kissi money could be carried by bundling the bars together and tying them with a leather strap. To give you an idea of how much Kissi money you needed to get by in West Africa, a cow would set you back about one hundred bundles of Kissi money, or you could walk away with a virgin bride for the low, low cost of two hundred bundles of Kissi money.

Eventually Kissi money was phased out in favor of other currencies in West Africa. But for a period of time in West African history, if you wanted to pay for something, you'd better have the Kissi!

As strange as the Kissi economy seems to us today, heaven's economy for payment for sins is even stranger! It's always been about *blood*. Whether it was Old Testament sacrifices and animal blood or the New Testament sacrifice and Jesus's blood, there's one thing we know for sure: heaven has a *blood*-based economy for sins.

Heaven's Blood Economy

For thousands of years, Israel was keenly aware of heaven's blood economy. Year after year, the Israelites offered blood sacrifices for their sins. On the Day of Atonement, they didn't offer long lists of apologies or make promises to do better. Of course, they were sorry for their sins and they didn't want to repeat the offenses. But they were well aware of what brought them forgiveness: blood, and blood alone.

Ask any devout Jew of that day what gave them relief from the burden of guilt over their sins, and you'd get the same answer every time—the blood of bulls and goats. They knew that heaven did not hear them because of their wailing. Their God was not merciful to them because of their begging and pleading for forgiveness. No, for thousands of years an elaborate system had been in place to deal with sins. It involved an altar, the slaughter of hoofed animals, and a special Day of Atonement on which all this took place, once a year. That was the God-ordained way to feel better about your sins—through blood.

Heaven's economy hasn't changed; it's still the same today. While it's certainly healthy for us to be sorry for our sins, the blood economy is still the only system heaven honors today. Only blood brings forgiveness. Not apologies. Not asking for forgiveness. Not our pleading or begging.

Now, take a moment to contemplate these questions:

- Which blood sacrifice makes me forgiven of my sins?
- For how many of my sins was it offered?
- Will the sacrifice ever be repeated?
- If not, then what should I conclude about its effectiveness the first time?

We are *not* people who are being forgiven progressively as we ask for it. We are forgiven people, period. Why? Because our forgiveness comes only through blood sacrifice, nothing else.

Cleansed "Once for All"

While the old covenant involved thousands of blood sacrifices repeated each year, the new covenant involves the one-time sacrifice of Jesus. As we see in the book of Hebrews, the old covenant involved people getting forgiven progressively, year after year. The new covenant involves people getting forgiven and cleansed once for all:

> The law is only a shadow of the good things that are coming—not the realities themselves. For this reason it can never, *by the same sacrifices repeated endlessly year after year*, make perfect those who draw near to worship. Otherwise, would they not have stopped being offered? *For the worshipers would have been cleansed once for all*, and would no longer have felt guilty for their sins. (Heb. 10:1–2)

Under the old way, the work was never done. The priests of old continually offered the same sacrifices, again and again, that could never take away their sins (10:11) or make anyone perfectly cleansed (10:1). Those sacrifices were actually an annual reminder of sins (10:3). Heaven wanted Israel to have an annual reminder of the unfinished business that wouldn't be settled until Calvary.

Not until the perfect lamb, the Lamb of God himself, was sacrificed could the Jews fold up shop on their sacrifices of old. Then there would be no reason to continue them. After all, why have a system of ongoing sacrifices and ongoing forgiveness if we've already been forgiven "once for all" (10:10)? It just makes no sense.

And that's exactly what the cross accomplished for us—"once for all" forgiveness. So today, we can fold up shop on any other methods to get forgiven, get cleansed, and stay that way. Instead, we can look back on and celebrate the one-time blood sacrifice of Jesus Christ. It's a sacrifice that needs no repeating.

What does this mean? It means we're not people who are progressively being forgiven, year after year or day after day. No, that was the old covenant way. Our new covenant forgiveness has *already* been accomplished.

It really is finished.

The Martha Syndrome

Jewish priests couldn't sit down on the job. For thousands of years, a chair was not even permitted in the tabernacle or temple. God's intent was to forever imprint on the Jewish mind the image of ongoing work, unfinished business.

> Day after day *every priest stands* and performs his religious duties; again and again he offers the same sacrifices, which can never take away sins. But when this priest had offered for all time one sacrifice for sins, *he sat down* at the right hand of God. (Heb. 10:11–12)

Israel never felt that their sins were completely hidden from the eyes of God. There were always more sins to atone for, more sins to cover. And the priest was continually standing, offering the same animal sacrifices over and over.

Then came Jesus, who did the unthinkable—he offered the sacrifice of himself, once, and then *sat down* at the right hand of God. The significance of this is astronomical. For the first time in human history, a priest who had offered a sacrifice for sins was sitting down on the job!

> The Son is the radiance of God's glory and the exact representation of his being, sustaining all things by his powerful word. After he had provided purification for sins, *he sat down* at the right hand of the Majesty in heaven. (Heb. 1:3)

Christ is seated right next to God, and they both know full well that all sacrifice for sins is over. So the question is this: What are we doing with regard to our sins? Are we suffering from the Martha Syndrome—running around the kitchen, trying to get things clean and get things right for Jesus? Or are we like Mary, resting at the feet of Jesus, relaxing in a seated position with him (Luke 10:38–42)?

The work is finished. We are forgiven. We are cleansed. And how we respond to this truth changes everything.

Perfected, for All Time!

While the sacrifice of Jesus Christ was two thousand years ago, its effects were all-encompassing. Our past, present, and future sins were all taken away at the cross. Yes, even our next sin—the one we haven't even contemplated doing yet—was included in the work of the cross! Heaven looked down the timeline of human history and, seeing all our sins, took them away through the blood of Jesus.

Just think about it. How many of your sins were in the future when Christ died? All of them. Is there any verse that says sins before salvation and sins after salvation are treated differently by the cross? Of course not! By that flawed logic, the gospel *gets worse after salvation*, with the cross having a weaker effect on sins after conversion. Ridiculous! By that thinking, we'd be better off becoming Christians on our deathbeds so that we don't build up too many sins as saved people.

The finished work of Jesus is simpler than all of that. The fact is that our entire lifetime of sins was taken away two thousand years ago. We are not people who *can* be forgiven or *might* be forgiven or *will* be forgiven. We are forgiven people, forever:

> By one offering [Jesus] has *perfected for all time* those who are sanctified. (Heb. 10:14 NASB)

And that's heaven's next message to us.

HEAVEN SPEAKS

You don't picture me offering myself over and over for your sins. But you do sometimes fall into the trap of thinking that I'm forgiving you little by little on an ongoing basis. That's the same as thinking I die again and again. After all, only my blood brought you forgiveness.

The whole idea of the cross was that it's finished. So now I'm asking you to sit and relax with me. Behold my finished work! Take in all that I've done for you. You don't have to ask for what I've already given. I carried out my plan to forgive you before you even knew to ask.

While the sacrifices of old were done over and over in man-made temples, I suffered outside the city gate and then entered heaven itself. When I sat down, it was something no former priest could do. For thousands of years, they remained standing, performing their religious duties over and over. But after I made purification for your sins, I sat down at Father's right hand.

So can you see the difference between the old way and my new way for you? You are a totally forgiven person, with no strings attached. That's the simple and profound truth of my finished work. I will never bear your sins again, not now and not when I return. I'm coming back to bring you salvation, the redemption of your body. Nothing else. Not judgment or punishment. I already judged your sins, and the punishment was death. I died in your place to take the judgment and all the punishment too. It's simple accounting. It's payment in full with no debt remaining.

If you haven't settled into the finality of my one-time death for you, how will you move on to enjoy the reality of my resurrection life in you? I gave you peace with me, so you can now experience peace in me and my peace in you.

I love you. Believe in my love and be happy.

Jesus

Awakening TO HEAVEN

Jesus, my one and only High Priest, I see clearly now that you are not up in heaven dying over and over again. Instead, you are seated at Father's right hand. I accept your invitation to sit down with you and rest in the sufficiency of your one-time sacrifice. I agree with you, confessing that I am a forgiven person. Never again will I equate your blood with that of Old Testament animal sacrifices. My forgiveness is not ongoing, day after day. It is finished, once for all. I thank you for showing me the finality of the cross so that I can enjoy the reality of your resurrection life in me!

Heaven Speaks inspired by Hebrews 1:3; 4:10; 9:22, 25–26, 28; 10:10–12; 13:11–13; John 16:33; 19:30; Luke 10:41–42; Romans 5:1, 8, 10; 6:23; 8:23; 1 Peter 2:24; Colossians 2:13–14.

11

For just $1.99 you can download "Confession: A Roman Catholic App" on your smartphone. The creators of this bestselling app claim it's an inexpensive and convenient way to get right and stay right with God, using your mobile device. The user checks various boxes under each of the Ten Commandments to keep a running tally of their sins so no sins remain unforgiven. While the Vatican seemed to support the idea at first, spokesperson Federico Lombardi later told the media, "Under no circumstance is it possible to 'confess by iPhone.'"[*]

Some of us may find the idea of confession through a mobile app nothing short of laughable. We imagine masses of people out there trying to

---

[*] AFP, "Vatican Bans Confession by iPhone," February 9, 2011, http://www.google.com/hostednews/afp/article/ALeqM5g7qz1gnBS NHb1Z2LjksqxOW8GdkA?docId=CNG.bf09dbb285cf3ab677f4bc7 d6d271075.2b1.

tally all their sins and frantically checking boxes to keep up with all of them. It's so difficult to stay right with God that they need a mobile device to pull it off!

But while we chuckle at this method, it seems that many of us Christians have bought into something quite similar. Maybe we don't download the app, but we still believe it's our ongoing verbal confession to God that keeps us forgiven and cleansed. Forgetting God's blood-based economy that made us forgiven and cleansed "once for all," we opt for a *word*-based economy that turns our confession into the catalyst for God forgiving and cleansing us. And for many of us, it seems that a misinterpretation of one single verse—1 John 1:9—has been the entire basis for this belief system.

CONDITIONAL FORGIVENESS?

First John 1:9 says, "*If we confess our sins*, he is faithful and just to forgive us our sins and to cleanse us from all unrighteousness" (ESV). It seems pretty clear, doesn't it? If we don't confess each and every sin, we won't be forgiven by God—right?

Multiple books and teachings on forgiveness have camped on this single verse as the landmark passage for justifying a two-tiered belief system concerning forgiveness. The system goes something like this: Yes, we have been forgiven (past tense), and yes, it was once for all. But that's from God's eternal vantage point. First John 1:9 was written to tell us Christians that we need to remember to confess each and every sin throughout our lives in order to remain forgiven and cleansed down here on planet earth. If we refuse or fail to confess all of our sins, then they remain between us and God, and we are consequently "out of fellowship." Some even go further by claiming that God can't hear our prayers if there are any unconfessed sins in our lives.

THE FIRST HERESY

To dispel this popular, "me-centered" teaching on forgiveness, let's examine the true context of 1 John 1:9.

First, this chapter opens with frequent mentions of our physical senses. John says that he and his fellow disciples saw Jesus, heard Jesus, and touched Jesus. John uses these words to indicate that Jesus was a real physical being, not just spiritual. This was a critical piece of information to the early church, since early forms of Gnostic heresy were claiming that Jesus was *only spiritual* in nature. So in addressing this heresy, John is careful to emphasize Jesus's physicality.

It's the most natural thing in the world for us to assume that John is writing *only* to Christians. But you can't be a Christian and believe that Jesus didn't come in the flesh (2 John 1:7). So in this chapter, John is addressing the *un*belief of Gnostics in the early church.

Why does this matter for the infamous 1 John 1:9 verse? Because John is still addressing Gnostic heresy throughout *the entire chapter*, not just in the first few verses.

The Second Heresy

The second heresy John addresses is the Gnostic idea that sin wasn't real or didn't matter. Notice that John is addressing people who were saying, "We have no sin" (1 John 1:8) and "We have not sinned" (1:10). So what's John's solution to their heresy? Simple. He tells them:

> *If we confess our sins*, he is faithful and just to forgive us our sins and to cleanse us from all unrighteousness. (1:9 ESV)

John is using "we" to politely combat Gnostic heresy by essentially saying, "If any one of us hanging out with the church is claiming to have never sinned, then we lie and do not practice the truth. In fact, we are making God a liar, and his Word has no place in our lives. But if we confess our sins, then he will forgive us and cleanse us from *all* unrighteousness."

Notice that John uses the word *all* to describe the kind of forgiveness and cleansing we receive once we have admitted our sins and accepted Jesus Christ (the living Word) into our lives. Also notice that John says his purpose in addressing his readers is so that they can have fellowship:

> We proclaim to you what we have seen and heard, *so that you also may have fellowship with us.* And *our* fellowship is with the Father and with his Son, Jesus Christ. (1:3)

Many people reading the letter did not yet have fellowship with Christians, or with the Father, or with Jesus Christ. In other words, many reading the letter were not yet saved. John's hope was that they would, by reading and understanding what he wrote, come to salvation. How could they come to salvation? Specifically, by confessing that Jesus did come in the flesh, that sin is real, and that Jesus is the answer to their sin problem. When they do this, Jesus forgives and cleanses them from *all* unrighteousness—past, present, and future sins.

John never intended for Christians to use verse 9 to build a theology of one-by-one confession to get one-by-one forgiveness of sins. That's *old* covenant forgiveness dressed up in 1 John 1:9 clothing!

The Conclusion Clarified

So does that mean the epistle of 1 John was written exclusively to lost people? Of course not! Epistles in the New Testament were written so that they could be publicly read to large groups of people. Some were saved; some were lost. Notice that John opens his *second* chapter with the words, "My little children" (2:1 ESV). John clearly means Christians here, as he even goes on to say the opposite of 1 John 1:9! Chapter 2 verse 12 says we "have been forgiven" (past tense). It describes our forgiveness as a completed act, not something that is dependent on anything like confession. So in this epistle, John addresses both groups—the lost and the saved.

Confession is not a formula to get forgiven and stay forgiven as a Christian. In fact, heaven announces the opposite—we have been forgiven and made holy "once for all" (Heb. 10:10) and "by one offering He has perfected for all time those who are sanctified" (Heb. 10:14 NASB).

So let's confess our sins. Let's agree with God that sin is wrong. Let's agree with God about everything. But let's not belittle the blood of Christ! The blood of Christ cleansed us from every sin imaginable. It's not about our ability to remember every sin and confess them all. It's about Jesus's blood shed two thousand years ago. And it is finished.

Wow! Now, that's great news we can really celebrate. And that's just what heaven would have us do—celebrate.

HEAVEN SPEAKS

I have forgiven you for my name's sake. There's nothing else that needs to be done to make it so. No asking, no pleading, no begging—it is finished. You've been washed. You've been justified. You've been sanctified. Yes, even while your behavior is under construction, being sanctified little by little, you as a person have already been fully set apart, sanctified for me.

My forgiveness is real, and my forgiveness is now. So you live in a permanently cleansed state. I don't want you to continue on feeling guilty for your sins. Regret them, yes. Turn away from them, yes. But I have cleansed you once for all so that you need not feel the weight of them. I want you motivated by my love, not by guilt.

Remember that I canceled your debt against me. I bought you and reconciled you completely to me, not counting one single sin against you. They've all been taken off the books, and you don't owe me.

The only way you can enjoy the present with me is to acknowledge my work in the past.

I took away your sins so that you could walk with me, fixing your eyes on my smile toward you. You'll only get tripped up as you look back at where you once were instead of where I'm taking you.

If you find yourself lacking the character and self-control you need, simply take in a fresh reminder of my "once for all" sacrifice. As you remember that you are clean and holy before me, you'll find yourself gravitating toward clean thinking and holy, set-apart choices. And as you recognize your closeness to me, you will naturally act like me.

I love you, and I delight in all that you are.

Jesus

Awakening TO HEAVEN

Thank you, Jesus, for taking away my sins—past, present, and future. I see your finished work for what it truly is. I believe it was enough.

Now that I see just how forgiven I am, I can only be eternally grateful for what you've done for me. Thank you for making me clean and drawing me close to you forever and no matter what. Your love and forgiveness inspire me to live the way you've intended—from my unbreakable union with you. I look forward to waking up every day and walking with you, in confidence. You've given me a new hope, a new joy. You've given me the greatest gift I could ever receive. You've given me yourself.

I love you too.

Heaven Speaks inspired by 1 John 2:12; 1 Corinthians 6:11, 20; 7:23; 1 Peter 1:15; 3:18; Hebrews 4:16; 7:27; 10:2; 12:2; 2 Corinthians 5:19; 7:10; Romans 6:12; Revelation 2:5; Psalm 103:11–12; John 1:29; 17:24; 2 Peter 1:8–9; Proverbs 23:7; Ephesians 3:12.

12

I used to get pretty anxious about conducting wedding ceremonies. I think it came down to not wanting to disappoint those mothers. You know, the mother of the groom and, more importantly, the mother of the bride! With all the formality and expectations, my stomach would just start churning. I always made it through, but I inevitably wrestled with the whole ordeal.

But all of this changed recently when my friend Thomas asked me to preside over the ceremony in which he would marry his fiancée, Marisa. When I arrived at the wedding rehearsal, I was met with an unusual request. The bride and groom wanted me to perform the ceremony while standing on the floor, looking up at them on stage, with my back to the audience.

I thought the idea was peculiar at first. But given all the money they'd spent on such a beautiful gown for Marisa and a handsome tuxedo for Thomas, they wanted to show them off during the ceremony. So they wanted to face the audience and thereby keep the focus on them. After all, *they* were the ones getting married!

When it came time for the ceremony, Marisa walked down the aisle, and her father placed her hand in Thomas's hand. Then I stepped down off the stage and turned my back to the audience, while Thomas and Marisa took their spots on stage facing us all.

I'll never forget that moment. What would ordinarily have been a nerve-racking event for me now seemed much more relaxed. No longer was I staring out at a sea of eyeballs that were staring right back at me. Nor was I peering into the mother of the bride's face to see if she was satisfied with how things were going. Instead, I focused my attention exclusively on the bride and groom. And from that day forward, no matter what position I stand in during a wedding, I've learned to keep my focus where it should be—on the bride and groom, because it's *their* day!

My struggle with weddings reminds me of the nerve-racking distractions we may encounter spiritually. We worry about what people think of us, fixing our eyes on them and living to please them. We worry about our sins, fixing our eyes on them and living in guilt. But all the while, God has called us to fixate on one thing alone—not our sins, not our performance, but Jesus. We are the bride, and Christ is the bridegroom. It is our spiritual union with Jesus Christ that has taken center stage. So here are some questions for you: What are you looking at? Is your attention focused on how you've been doing lately? Or on what other people think of you? Are you focused on yourself and your sins? If so, there's a simple fix: turn your back to all those distractions and look up! Set your mind on things above where Christ is seated. He deserves our full attention. And when we give him the focus he deserves, we find ourselves at peace, at rest, and able to enjoy the celebration!

Forgiven, Period

Colossians tells us that "he *forgave* us all our sins" (2:13). Ephesians tells us that "God *forgave* you" (4:32). Hebrews tells us that "these *have been forgiven*" (10:18). First John tells us that "your sins *have been forgiven* you for His name's sake" (2:12 NASB). In all of these cases, our forgiveness is expressed in the past tense as a completed action. The simple message from heaven is that God will never forgive us any more than we've already been forgiven. He doesn't have to, because he forgave us "*all* our sins" (Col. 2:13) the first time!

No matter how much we might be tempted to dismiss this new covenant message as "cheap grace" or "a license to sin," the blood of Jesus Christ will always be staring us in the face. What did it accomplish? How many of our sins did it take away? And do I really believe that I need to do something further to "activate" or "appropriate" it? Even Old Testament Jews didn't buy into that for the blood of bulls and goats. Once those animals were slaughtered, that was it. No activation needed. No appropriation necessary. It was finished, until next year. How much *more* does the blood of Christ cleanse us *once for all* and give us a good conscience before God (Heb. 9:14; 10:2)?

We are forgiven people, period.

STOP, DROP, AND ROLL!

Now, let's talk more about confession, since we've already seen what it's *not* for. It's not for obtaining new portions of forgiveness and cleansing. But what *is* it for?

James 5:16 tells us it's healthy to confess our sins to each other and pray for each other. So that God will forgive us? No, he already has! But we share our struggles with trusted friends so that they can pray for us and encourage us with the truth of our forgiveness and our new identity. As they help us fill our minds with truth, there is hope for change.

The opening of our lives to other people doesn't throw heaven into motion to forgive us. It doesn't put Christ back up on the cross to die again. And it doesn't appropriate anything. *It just makes sense.*

Given that we're not supposed to live life as "lone ranger" Christians, and given that we are forgiven and accepted by God, why not open up to those we trust and seek their prayers and counsel?

Whenever I teach on total forgiveness, people always end up asking, "Well, then what *should* I do when I sin?" One of my favorite responses is, "Stop, drop, and roll. This also works well in a fire." But seriously, what should we do? Stop sinning, of course, and get away from the temptation. It doesn't take a rocket scientist to realize that God's primary concern when we sin is that we not be damaged by it and that we not get mired in it. Turning from sin is healthy and fitting given that we are new creations in Jesus Christ. As Paul puts it, "How can we live in it any longer?" (Rom. 6:2).

Notice Paul's counsel to the man in the early church who was stealing (Eph. 4:28). Paul essentially tells him, "Stop stealing, get a job, and give some to the poor." Now, there's a practical response that is concerned with the man's future. There's no condemning of the man. There's no getting him to go through a cleansing ritual. The solution is simple: stop sinning, and act differently next time. That's the simple answer to what we should do when we sin.

FOCUS ON FORGIVENESS

God wasn't naïve in giving us this new covenant. Each aspect of it works to empower us to live like the new creations that we are. So when it comes to the issue of forgiveness, let's not insult the Spirit of grace. God knows exactly how to motivate us from the heart to live upright lives. Our total, unconditional forgiveness in no way hinders an upright life. In fact, we find that the opposite is true:

> But whoever does not have them [qualities such as love and self-control] is nearsighted and blind, *forgetting that they have been cleansed from their past sins*. (2 Pet. 1:9)

> Anyone who listens to the word but does not do what it says is like someone who looks at his face in a mirror and, after looking at himself, goes away and *immediately forgets what he looks like*. (James 1:23–24)

Remembering our totally cleansed state before God is what brings good qualities like kindness and love into our lives. If we lack these qualities and are not doers of the Word, then it's because we've simply forgotten who we are. We have forgotten our new identity as forgiven, holy saints.

This "once for all" forgiveness means that we can fix our eyes on Jesus, not on ourselves. In fact, the entirety of the gospel—forgiveness, freedom from law, acceptance, and intimacy with Christ—is designed to move us away from a focus on self. We need not inspect ourselves, analyze ourselves, or try to cleanse ourselves or make ourselves right. This was accomplished by Jesus. Our job today is to rest in his *finished* work that needs no repeat.

GROUNDHOG DAY

In the film *Groundhog Day*, Phil is a weatherman who is frustrated that he has to cover the same small-town story every year on Groundhog Day. Things get even worse for Phil when he wakes up the next day only to discover that it's Groundhog Day all over again. The same thing happens the next day, and the next, and the next. Of course, comedy ensues as Phil repetitively struggles with the same events occurring over and over.

While this plot makes for a hilarious film, it's less than amusing to God when we envision his Son's sacrifice to be an ongoing affair. It seems obvious to us today that Jesus Christ died only once. He is not up in heaven dying over and over again. But two thousand years ago, this was a big deal emphasized by the apostles. In the book of Hebrews, it's expressed this way:

> Nor did he enter heaven to offer himself again and again, the way the high priest enters the Most Holy Place every year with blood that is not his own. Otherwise Christ would have had to suffer many times since the creation of the world. But he has appeared once for all at the culmination of the ages to do away with sin by the sacrifice of himself. (Heb. 9:25–26)

In the seventh chapter of Hebrews, the writer also says that "[Christ] does not need to offer sacrifices day after day" and that "he sacrificed for their sins once for all" (v. 27). Why emphasize this point? It goes back to that heavenly economy that the Jews of that day understood so well. Here's the logic: if blood is the only thing that brings forgiveness, and if Jesus died only once and will never die again, then I am as forgiven right now as I will ever be!

This was a huge deal for the early church, and it's still a big deal today. Many Christians are still peddling another economy for sins. We're saying that we're forgiven only when we ask. We're saying that we're cleansed only when we confess. But the simple truth is that we have been forgiven and cleansed *once for all*. And in heaven, there's no Groundhog Day.

So have your senses been awakened to heaven's one-time solution for sins? Can you see the *finished* work of Jesus in all its clarity?

Here's heaven's next message to us.

HEAVEN SPEAKS

I will never deal with your sins again. I dealt with them once, and that is enough. Father received payment in full, and for you, the sin issue is over. This means that I will return for you without making reference to your sins. I remember them no more. There is no punishment left for you, not now or in the future.

When you sin, you may look for some way to get back into my good graces. What I'm telling you is that you are already and always there. I don't want you to make attempts to add to my work. Instead, I want you to celebrate what I accomplished on Calvary. I purchased a place for you, a permanent place in me that is never in jeopardy.

I also want to protect you from the earthly consequences of sin. The outcome is never good. So the goal of my counsel is to save you from wasting time and energy walking after the flesh. What should you do when you sin? Turn away from it and choose to walk with me and live from me. Then you won't gratify the desires of the flesh. I'm only concerned about your future, your next steps, not about your failures in the past.

Remember that my grace doesn't just manifest itself in the form of forgiveness. My grace has also equipped you to live differently. As you remember how my grace transformed you, you will walk in that way. It's simple, not complicated. As a person thinks, so will they act. Just allow my Spirit to remind you, over and over, of the beautiful new creation that I have made you into. Total forgiveness and a brand-new identity are part of your heavenly inheritance, to be enjoyed here and now.

I love you, and I only want my best for you.

Jesus

Awakening TO HEAVEN

Jesus, thank you that I no longer have to wonder where I stand with you or try to get back into fellowship with you. I am in! You ask me to walk with you, step by step, making wise choices in dependency on you. How can my heart not leap with joy in response to someone who has loved me, forgiven me, and accepted me the way you do? There simply is no better life than the life you have

shared with me. Thank you for allowing me the privilege of being in your presence each and every day, without interruption.
I love you so.

Heaven Speaks inspired by Romans 6:9–10, 12, 21; 8:1; 11:29; Hebrews 9:28; 10:17; 13:5; 1 John 4:18; 2 Timothy 2:13; Galatians 3:3; 5:16; Acts 26:18; 1 Peter 4:2; Ephesians 4:28; Titus 2:11–12; Proverbs 23:7; Colossians 2:13.

13

In Luke 15, Jesus tells the story of the prodigal
son, a young man who asks his father for his
inheritance early so he can enjoy life in the fast
lane. Then he goes out and squanders everything
he's been given. Once a famine hits the land, the
young man is forced to take a job feeding pigs.
As he's sitting there in the muck and the mire, he
begins thinking, "How many of my father's hired
servants have food to spare, and here I am starving
to death!" (v. 17). So he decides to try going home
and begins rehearsing what he'll say when he gets
there: "Father, I have sinned against heaven and
against you. I am no longer worthy to be called
your son; make me like one of your hired servants"
(vv. 18–19). But as the young man approaches his
father's estate, here's how the story concludes:

> But while he was still a long way off, his father
> saw him and was filled with compassion for him;

he ran to his son, threw his arms around him and kissed him. The son said to him, "Father, I have sinned against heaven and against you. I am no longer worthy to be called your son."

But the father said to his servants, "Quick! Bring the best robe and put it on him. Put a ring on his finger and sandals on his feet. Bring the fattened calf and kill it. Let's have a feast and celebrate. For this son of mine was dead and is alive again; he was lost and is found." So they began to celebrate. (vv. 20–24)

The son had a penitent speech prepared. He was ready to be relegated to the role of a second-class citizen—a servant, no longer a son. But his father wouldn't have it. Did you notice the father's response? Not even entertaining the idea, the father says, "Quick! Bring the best robe" (v. 22). The father wishes to clothe him, not condemn him. Then he says, "Let's have a feast" (v. 23).

Where's the asking for forgiveness? And where's the granting of it only after being asked? I love this story because the father is operating under the assumption that the son is already forgiven and that the son should realize this. Upon his son's return, the father's first words relate to the future, not the past.

Often we feel like the prodigal son. We think God needs us to ask him to forgive us, and then and only then does he forgive. But does the Bible really teach new covenant Christians to *ask* for forgiveness? Or is God like the father in this story, operating under the assumption that we are already forgiven?

THE LORD'S PRAYER

There's no question that Jesus tells his disciples to ask God for forgiveness when they pray. His words are recorded in perhaps the most well-known passage in the Bible, one that is recited at a wide array of events from church services to royal weddings. That's right, I'm talking about the Lord's Prayer (Matt. 6:9–13).

We all know it, right? Probably even in the original King James: "Forgive us our trespasses as we forgive those . . ." But despite our familiarity with this passage, the context of the Lord's Prayer may surprise us if we slow down long enough to read the whole thing and consider what it's really saying.

First, we need to take note of the historical and biblical context of the Lord's Prayer. Jesus was telling his Jewish contemporaries how to pray *before* he went to the cross and died for their sins. That can't be stressed enough—that Jesus's prayer involving forgiveness was given as a model before he achieved total forgiveness on Calvary.

Remember that a covenant only goes into effect when there has been a *death* (Heb. 9:16–17). So was the new covenant in effect at the time of that prayer? No, not yet. And Galatians tells us that Jesus was *born under the law* (Gal. 4:4). So it was not Jesus's birth but his death that initiated the new covenant. Why is this so important? Because this is clearly a prayer offered under the old covenant.

The Clear Condition

Keeping this in mind, take a moment to reread a key part of the prayer. Notice that it doesn't just say, "Forgive us our debts." No, it says something much more specific. It says, "Forgive us our debts *as we also have forgiven* our debtors" (Matt. 6:12). Essentially, Jesus is telling his Jewish listeners that they are free to ask God for forgiveness, but they should ask God for forgiveness only in the same proportion to which they have forgiven other people!

Not sure that Jesus really means that? Well, check out the conclusion to his prayer, which is not often included in our recitations:

> For *if you forgive other people* when they sin against you, your heavenly Father will also forgive you. But *if you do not forgive others* their sins, your Father will not forgive your sins. (Matt. 6:14–15)

Sound conditional to you? It is—very conditional. It's quite clear that if you do your part, God will do his. But if you don't do your part, God won't do his. So our own forgiveness is wrapped up in our performance as a forgiver of other people. Sound like the gospel you hear every Sunday? I hope not!

If you were to review any sermon delivered by the apostles in the book of Acts and all the verses in the New Testament epistles, you wouldn't find a single teaching similar to what Jesus said at the conclusion of this prayer. Not once would you find that our forgiveness from God is dependent on our forgiving of other people.

In fact, we find the opposite. Both Ephesians 4:32 and Colossians 3:13 say the same thing—that we should forgive other people, because God *already* forgave us. We don't forgive to get forgiven. We forgive because we've already been forgiven. We're designed to pass it on.

RAISING THE BAR

So why does Jesus appear to teach something that contradicts what Paul later tells the Ephesians and Colossians? Aren't they both teaching under the same new covenant? No, remember that the new covenant began at Jesus's death. So the Lord's Prayer is an "old" prayer that condemns.

We asked similar questions earlier in this book: Why would Jesus tell the rich man to sell everything? Is that really the way into the kingdom? Why would he tell others to pluck out their eye and cut off their hand? Is that really how to avoid hell? Recall that Jesus was raising the standard of the law to a place of impossibility. The law was already impossible to truly keep, but many Jews thought they were doing just fine. Then Jesus came along talking about removing body parts and selling everything, and people took notice.

When it came to forgiveness, it was no different. Upon hearing Jesus praying this way, they probably thought, "God will forgive me to the same degree that I've forgiven others? Ouch! That's not very promising. I'm going to need another way if I want to survive!" And that's exactly what they got through Calvary—a *new* way.

THE BIG PICTURE

Do you see the big picture? Jesus's sacrifice brought us "once for all" forgiveness and cleansing (Heb. 9:26–27; 10:1–3; 1 Peter 3:18). Jesus did more than cover our sins; he took them away forever (John 1:29; Heb. 10:11–13; 1 John 3:5). By his one blood offering, he made us perfectly cleansed forever (Heb. 10:14). Our forgiveness is announced as a past tense, completed action (Eph. 4:32; Col. 2:13–14; Heb. 10:17–18; 1 John 2:12). And because he remembers our sins no more (Heb. 10:17), he will return for us without reference to our sins (Heb. 9:28).

We can either build our beliefs concerning forgiveness on an old covenant prayer of despair and a verse taken out of context (1 John 1:9), or we can build them on the dozens of New Testament passages that announce that Jesus took away our sins once for all, making us perfectly forgiven and cleansed before God. The choice is ours. One choice leads to intellectual gymnastics and the sense that we are never fully right with God. The other choice leads us to a place of spiritual rest in which we wake up every day and give thanks for the finished work of Jesus. Which do you think brings a smile to God's face and warms the heart of heaven?

Here's what heaven has to say about it.

HEAVEN SPEAKS

I know you want to experience my love. You want to flick a switch and feel it in every moment. But I've designed you to fluctuate. Your feelings come and go, and your thoughts ebb and flow. This makes life the adventure that it is, and it makes trust in my one-time sacrifice all the more exhilarating. So don't let your feelings tell you what to believe. My love is known and experienced in realizing what I've already done for you in taking away your sins.

My love is patient toward you. My love is kind toward you. Because of my love for you, I am never angered with you, nor do I keep any record of your wrongs. The message of the cross is my love in plain sight.

You don't need to ask, over and over, for what I have already given you. When you find yourself feeling dirty and distant and wondering where my love and forgiveness are, remember that I am experienced through truth. The magnificent reality is that my love for you never ceases. And my forgiveness of you has already taken place—you are forgiven now and for eternity.

In suffering my death for you and in giving my life to you, I'm shouting from the rooftops that I am for you. I have chosen to align myself with you, no matter what. I am on your team and in your corner. The gospel message is my way of demonstrating my deep love for you. This is why it will never grow old. The layers of its glory are infinitely deep, just as my love for you is infinitely deep. So when you experience those vacillations of the soul, just reflect on my finished work, and you'll remember how dearly I love you.

Jesus

Awakening TO HEAVEN

Jesus, teach me to turn to truth in times of trouble. I cry out to know and feel your love and forgiveness, but now I see how you've cried out to me in the gospel itself. Your finished work is the answer to my heartache. The lengths you went to in order to purchase me and own me speak volumes. I choose to thank you for what you've done through the cross and resurrection rather than perpetually asking for what I already have in you. Thank you for forgiving me once for all. Thank you for aligning my heart with yours. I love you more than I can even express.

Heaven Speaks inspired by 2 Corinthians 3:10–11; 5:7; Romans 5:8, 10; 1 Corinthians 1:18; 6:17; 13:4–8; Ephesians 2:6; 4:32; John 4:24; 8:32; 10:10; Psalm 136:1; Colossians 2:13; 3:12–13; 1 John 2:12; Hebrews 9:28; 13:5; Galatians 5:17; 2 Timothy 2:13.

14

There's a movie about a woman named Libby who is framed for her husband's murder. Libby is prosecuted for the crime and serves her time. But when she is released, she discovers that her husband is still alive and had concocted an elaborate scheme to fake his own death and frame her for the murder. The film then documents Libby's attempts to find her husband and kill him, knowing that she can't be prosecuted again. The title of the film, *Double Jeopardy*, refers to a law in the United States that stipulates a person cannot be tried twice for the same crime.

We respect the idea of double jeopardy within our judicial system, but we don't seem to understand it very well when it comes to the spiritual realm. While most Christians agree on the general idea that our sins were judged and punished at the cross, many of those same people simultaneously believe that we Christians are going to be judged for our sins upon Christ's return. The only problem with this is that these two ideas can't both be true. It cannot possibly be true that our sins are paid for in full, totally forgiven, forgotten, and taken away and at the same time be true that we will be judged for them. That'd be a case of double jeopardy.

The fact is that we were already judged for our sins. The verdict was guilty. The sentence was death. And that sentence was carried out on Calvary! This means we'll never be judged for our sins again, because it's already happened once, and now the Judge is satisfied. The punishment fit the crime.

Have you come to grips with the fact that God has let you off the hook for your sins? Or do you, in the back of your mind, still fear that you'll have to answer for your sins when you meet your Maker in the sky? The simple truth is that God's perfect love, as demonstrated on the cross, drives out our fear. If we're living in fear of God, it's because we still think punishment is on its way:

> There is no fear in love. But perfect love drives out fear, because *fear has to do with punishment*. The one who fears is not made perfect in love. (1 John 4:18)

With regard to punishment, it is finished (John 19:30), and there is therefore now no condemnation of any kind for us (Rom. 8:1). Here's a verse that shouts as clearly as any that Jesus is returning to bring us *salvation*, nothing else:

> Christ also, having been offered once to bear the sins of many, will appear a second time for salvation *without reference to sin*, to those who eagerly await Him. (Heb. 9:28 NASB)

EGYPTIAN DOUBLE-CROSSER!

You may know the Old Testament account of when Moses approached Pharaoh and asked for the Israelites to be released from slavery in Egypt. Pharaoh heard Moses's request and, after the plagues, consented to let Israel go. So Moses made the necessary preparations, and the Israelites began their exodus out of Egypt. But not too long after Israel's departure, Pharaoh sent his soldiers after Israel, seeking to bring them back into captivity! Of course, Pharaoh's attempt ended in failure as the Red Sea swallowed up his soldiers.

When we consider the actions of Pharaoh, we inevitably conclude, "What a dirty double-crosser! First he says Israel can go free, but then he goes back on his word!" I find it interesting that we can clearly identify Pharaoh as a dirty double-crosser, but some of us ascribe these same characteristics to our heavenly Father! We do this as we say out of one side of our mouth that we are forgiven for all of our sins and then out of the other side of our mouth that we'll be judged for our sins upon Christ's return. Just as in Pharaoh's case, that'd be a dirty double-cross.

New covenant forgiveness means that the sin issue is over, once and for all. God will never, ever mention our sins again in any context. He remembers them no more (Heb. 8:12)!

THE LITMUS TEST

But what about our works being judged and rewards being given? Doesn't Paul talk about fire testing the quality of each person's work? Here's what he says:

> No one can lay any foundation other than *the one already laid, which is Jesus Christ.* If anyone builds on this foundation using gold, silver, costly stones, wood, hay or straw, their work will be shown for what it is, because the Day will bring it to light. It will be revealed with fire, and the fire will test the quality of each person's work. (1 Cor. 3:11–13)

There's no question that God cares about behavior and its source. However, it's not what the behavior looks like that determines its worth. It's the *foundation* for our behavior that will determine whether it will stand the test of time. Was a certain action done in dependence on Christ? Or was it merely an expression of human effort? I think we'll be surprised as millions of sermons and philanthropic efforts are burned up alongside ugly-looking acts of the flesh. Meanwhile, other less-visible acts of love will stand the test of time because their source was Jesus Christ. It's all about the foundation.

This litmus test (or appraisal) at the end of the ages is about God celebrating the work of his Son. Any works that were done in the energy of the flesh will be disposed of so that all may rejoice with an unobstructed view of what God has accomplished throughout history.

HEAVENLY REWARD$?

It's often taught that we Christians should live uprightly in order to collect many rewards (plural) in heaven. What I find amusing about this teaching is that it supposes that we'll get rewards like multiple crowns, pockets full of jewels, and more square footage for our heavenly crib. Meanwhile, Paul writes that we shouldn't add to the foundation of Christ with anything else (1 Cor. 3:11–13)! Instead, Jesus is the foundation, and it's all about him from start to finish. Then, some of us turn right around and think that we can expect *what* in heaven? A fine assortment of gold and costly stones with our names engraved on them? Some of us Christians criticize Muslims who believe themselves to be earning virgins in heaven, yet we may essentially believe the same thing, only we're substituting wealth for sex as the prize in focus.

Yes, the Scriptures teach that we have a heavenly reward (singular, not plural) awaiting us. But since everything else is garbage next to knowing Christ Jesus, what else could our reward be if not *knowing him*?

> What is more, I consider everything a loss because of the surpassing worth of *knowing Christ Jesus my Lord*, for whose sake I have lost all things. *I consider them garbage*, that I may gain Christ. (Phil. 3:8)

Although we're not face-to-face yet, we can experience some of this heavenly reward while here on earth. When we pass our time continually walking after the flesh, we miss out on the privilege of expressing Jesus. But when we walk in dependency on the resurrection life of Jesus Christ within us, we experience the heavenly reward of knowing him right here and now! This is heaven's next message to us.

HEAVEN SPEAKS

My countenance is always toward you, and you have peace with me. I won't allow anything to separate you from the fullness of my love. And you don't need to bother entertaining fear about a future judgment, as I have set you free from the law of sin and death. Yes, sin deserves death, but through my own death, I have reconciled you, once and for all. Don't you see the great lengths I went to in order to make certain you'd enjoy an eternal reward with me?

Now that you are free to fail, my desire is for you to open up to me and share with me your innermost thoughts. I sympathize with your weaknesses, as I know what it's like to be tempted in every way. When you approach me, you'll find nothing but mercy and grace. You can talk to me with total confidence that I have already accepted you, fully and completely.

Upon my return, none of this will change. You will not face any judgment for your sins. Instead, I will wipe away every tear from your eyes, and you will experience no sorrow, only the joys of eternity with me. So there is no reason to fear my return. Fear comes from wrong ideas about judgment and punishment. But my perfect love has the power to drive away all your fears.

Whether you realize it or not, my grace is all around you, even now. There is grace behind you, and it has healed you from your past. My grace also goes before you, as I have already removed your future sins as far as the east is from the west. There is grace on your left and grace on your right. There is grace above you and grace beneath you. You are swimming in so much grace, and it will never run out. I have lavished you with my grace so that you might fall in love with me.

I love you, and I am your great reward.

Jesus

Awakening TO HEAVEN

Thank you, Jesus, for freeing me from the fear of judgment. I've often wondered why I couldn't sense a closer intimacy with you. Now I realize that I have been double-minded in my thinking. Because you have forgiven me, cleansed me, and taken away my sins forever, you will never refer to them again. I agree that the punishment that fell on you is enough and that I will never suffer punishment for my sins. You even allow me to enjoy the heavenly reward of knowing you for eternity, a reward I can participate in now. Thank you, Jesus, for opening my eyes to see your finished work in all its glory.

   I love you.

Heaven Speaks inspired by Numbers 6:26; Romans 5:1–2, 10; 6:23; 8:2, 38–39; 1 John 4:17–18; Colossians 1:22; 3:24; 2 Corinthians 5:18; Matthew 5:11–12; Revelation 11:18; 21:4; 1 Corinthians 6:12; 10:23; Galatians 5:13; 1 Thessalonians 5:17; Hebrews 4:15–16; 9:28; Ephesians 1:6–8; 1 Peter 2:24; Psalm 103:12.

SMELL
THE FRAGRANT
AROMA OF CHRIST

For we are to God the pleasing
aroma of Christ among those
who are being saved and
those who are perishing.

2 Corinthians 2:15

15

I'm doing everything I can think of, but I see no real change in my life."

Michael sat across from me at a local coffee shop, so full of frustration that it was leaking out around the edges. He had grown up in church. He went to a Christian high school and then to a Christian university. He was even the chaplain of his Christian fraternity. And Michael had immersed himself in Christian literature for years, reading all the popular Christian living titles.

Still, something was missing. Something big.

"Tell me a little about your spiritual history," I began.

"I devoted my life to God's service when I was very young. I've been going to church services and Bible studies my whole life. I've always wanted to live a good Christian life, but I guess I just don't feel like I have any power to live that way."

"How did you become a Christian?" I asked.

"I grew up in the church and always knew about Jesus, ever since I can remember."

"How would you describe what it means to be a Christian?" I asked.

"Well, you believe in Jesus and that he died on the cross, and you devote your life to obeying his Word."

"What if I told you that's not what a Christian is?" I persisted.

"What do you mean?" Michael asked.

"A Christian is not someone who devotes their life to obeying God's Word. God can't use our devotion or our life, for that matter. Being a Christian is not about giving our life to serving God; it's about God doing away with our life and giving *his* life to us!"

"I've never thought about it that way before," he said.

"Michael, no amount of Bible reading or service projects brings the change I'm talking about. God is looking to be a new source of life to us. He invites us to receive Christ's resurrected life within us. That's what it means to be a Christian."

"I'm not sure I've ever heard it put that way before," Michael said.

"Would you say that you have the resurrected Christ living in you, Michael?"

"I don't know. I guess I don't think so."

"The Scriptures tell us that we can *know* that we have eternal life and that eternal life is found in Christ. If you have Christ himself, then you have eternal life. It sounds to me like you might want to know for sure that you have Christ in you, as your eternal life."

"Yes, I want to know for sure," he said.

"Why don't you take a moment and express to God your belief in Jesus's death *and resurrection?* Invite Jesus Christ to be the resurrection life and the power for change within you that you so desperately need."

Michael had merely devoted his own life to Christian service, when he really needed to receive Christ's resurrection life. This is the subtle but life-changing difference between commitment and surrender. Commitment occurs when a person believes they are strong and capable. Surrender is the opposite: we surrender when we feel that we have nothing more to give. That day, Michael surrendered his own efforts and allowed Someone else to be the source of change. A man who had spent his life in church services, in Christian schools, and in religious work finally saw his true need—life.

ETERNAL LIFE, THE PERSON

Everlasting life, of course, has no end. But, by definition, *eternal life* is a life with *no beginning* and no end. So who is the only one whose life has no beginning or end? Christ himself. Eternal life is not our life made better. Eternal life is not our life made longer. Eternal life is an altogether different life. Possessing eternal life actually means possessing Christ's resurrection life (1 John 5:12).

This is the same life that Adam and Eve walked away from in Eden when they chose to eat from a tree of morality and ethics. That day they gained a sense of good and evil, but what they lost was devastating: they lost *life*. In the absence of life, they began looking to do good and avoid evil. Doing good gave them a feeling of rightness, of Godlikeness. But morality and ethics are no substitute for displaying God's divine life.

LIFE, NOT RELIGION

Many years ago, I was enrolled in a religion course at my university. The professor teaching the course was well versed in the Scriptures. He knew the Bible better than anyone I had ever met. But after class one day he said something to me that I've not forgotten:

> You know, lots of students ask me where I'm at spiritually, on a personal level. And I've found over the years that if I tell my students that I am a "born-again Christian" who has received Christ

as my Lord and Savior, many of them warm up to me and even confide in me like a close friend. But if I admit to them that I don't have a clue what it means to be "born again" or to "receive Christ," I find they react very differently. I just don't get it.

This professor who knew so much about theological terminology, church history, and the Bible itself did not know what it means to possess life.

I share this true story to demonstrate that we can have well-informed religion without having life. We can have knowledge of Scripture without having life. We can even be preaching or prophesying in Jesus's name (Matt. 7:22) without actually having life. The most important realization a person can come to is this: we are not bad and in need of being good; we are dead and in need of *life*. Awakening to the difference between religion and life gives us our first hint of the fragrant aroma of Jesus Christ.

SAVED BY LIFE

Consider the situation in the early church. Most cities had one or two epistles at most, and some had none at all from which to study or even read. The vast majority of the people in that day were illiterate. A personal "quiet time" in God's Word was literally impossible. So how did they rock the world two thousand years ago without having the regular study time that so many of us Christians seem to measure ourselves by today? The answer is simple—*Christ's life in them*. It was Christ's life within them that motivated and animated them to walk in love and to speak the truth, even if it cost them their lives. He was their strength, their courage, and their peace.

Don't get me wrong. We are blessed to have the entire Word of God in print today. And we are blessed to be able to read it! But without any of these conveniences, the early church made the Christian life work and work well. They not only survived but also thrived, bearing fruit and reaching out to others. How did they attain to such a Christian life?

They attained to it as they realized that the Christian life is Christ's life. To live the Christian life means that we live *from* Christ himself. We need only have our spiritual senses awakened to the purpose of the resurrection. It is Christ *risen* that brings heaven to earth and puts God's life in our humanity. This is the one and only life we are designed to express!

THE SECRET FORMULA

In 1886, a medicinal chemist named John Pemberton concocted a beverage that would later come to be known as Coca-Cola. Since that time, the only official copy of the recipe has been allegedly stored in a bank vault, and the Coca-Cola Company has kept the secret ingredients of their world-renowned beverage under tight watch for more than 125 years.

At least, that was the case until recently when producers of the program *This American Life* at Chicago Public Radio claimed they accidentally discovered the secret recipe for Coke in a 1979 article in the *Atlanta Journal-Constitution*. The article, buried on page 28 of the newspaper, featured a photo of a handwritten recipe that is purported to contain the exact ingredients Pemberton prescribed for Coca-Cola.

What for so long had been shrouded in mystery appears to have now been revealed. Similarly, this message of "Christ in you" was a mystery kept hidden for so long, but it has now been revealed to us on this side of the cross:

> *The mystery that has been kept hidden for ages and generations*, but is now disclosed to the Lord's people. To them God has chosen to make known among the Gentiles the glorious riches of *this mystery, which is Christ in you*, the hope of glory. (Col. 1:26–27)

This mystery, now revealed, is *not* Christ "falling fresh" on us now and then. This mystery is *not*

Christ swooping down from heaven to visit with us in a church meeting or revival. No, this mystery is much greater than all of that. This mystery is Christ in us, twenty-four hours a day, seven days a week, without interruption. Christ is our one single hope of expressing heaven's glory here and now. He is the secret formula for living the Christian life, and he has been revealed!

Here is heaven's next message to us about this miraculous life.

HEAVEN SPEAKS

I died for your forgiveness, but I was raised to life for your justification. While you were reconciled through my death, you were actually saved through receiving my resurrection life. If I had not been raised from the dead, you would still be dead in your sins, and your faith would be pointless and pitiful. My resurrection is the very heart of the gospel message.

Your body is now my temple, and you are not your own. You belong to me, as I bought you for a great price. Therefore, honor me with your body as you offer it as a living sacrifice and reap the benefits of housing my Spirit within you. This is a most sensible and worshipful act that leads to my life expressed through you.

Clothe yourself with me, and you will see yourself being transformed by the renewing of your attitudes. Then it will become more and more obvious to you what my will is for your life—simply that you bear my fruit. As you clothe yourself with love, kindness, and gentleness, others will take notice that there is a peculiar hope within you. Be ready to share this hope.

I love you. And I am your unlimited source of life.

Jesus

Awakening TO HEAVEN

Thank you, Jesus, for imparting your resurrection life to me. As much as I value your death as the means to my forgiveness, I see now that it is your resurrection that saves me and makes me new. I look forward to the day when I receive a new resurrection body, but I thank you that here and now I have been transformed at the core. Teach me the full meaning of your resurrection so that I can enjoy a clean conscience from knowing my righteousness in you. Teach me the power of your resurrection life in me so that I can bear fruit in this life, loving others with the love that only comes from you. Remind me that

apart from you I can do nothing and that through you I am more than a conqueror.
I love you, Jesus.

Heaven Speaks inspired by Romans 4:25; 5:10; 8:11; 12:1–2; 13:14; 1 Corinthians 6:19–20; 15:17; Acts 17:32; 23:6; John 15:8; 1 Peter 3:15; Colossians 3:4.

16

At Christmas, we reflect on the fact that God would humble himself to the point of taking on real human flesh. Why did God go about saving us in this way? He could have beamed himself to earth to die on a cross, offering the blood sacrifice needed, and then beamed himself back up again. But instead, he came as a fragile, helpless baby and lived thirty-three years as someone fully God and fully human at the same time.

I believe he did this to demonstrate that *his divinity is 100 percent compatible with our humanity.* He wanted to announce that the life Adam lost in the Garden was on display again in the humanity of Jesus. Why? So that one day that same life could be on display in *us*!

The natural implication of this reality is that we can stop trying to imitate the actions of Jesus as recorded in the Gospels. Instead, we can allow the risen Christ, who is alive and living in us, to be himself in and through our unique personalities.

He is the only catalyst for anything of value in the Christian life.

Just imagine trying to imitate the historical Jesus! If we really tried to do such a thing, it would be a grand exercise in futility. Sometimes he called people snakes. Other times he was toppling furniture over in church. Still other times he was befriending prostitutes. Not to mention the times that he did things like walk on water and put mud in people's eyes!

How could we ever know how to imitate Jesus? We'd try to apply a pattern or set of principles to the Christian life, and the waters would only become murky. Why? Because we were never designed to treat Christianity like a religion, merely imitating a historical teacher. We were designed to house the Spirit of the Teacher and exude him from within. We were designed to partake of his divine nature (2 Pet. 1:4).

But as we seek to smell the fragrant aroma of Christ and have our spiritual senses awakened to his presence within us, it's only natural to wonder, "Do I just let go and let God? Is it all of him and *none* of me? How does letting Christ live through me really play out?"

THE WILDFIRE WITHIN

Recently, record wildfires consumed nearly 150,000 acres here in Texas. For days we went to bed (safely, a few hours away) assuming that our place would be burnt to the ground by morning. Thanks to some very brave firefighters, our neighborhood ended up untouched. But the fire destroyed more than 150 homes and two churches in surrounding areas, even as hundreds of firefighters fought to put it out. In the days that followed, our hearts sank as we drove around witnessing all the destruction the fire had left behind.

While fire normally consumes everything in its path, there's one story in the Bible where it didn't. You may know the story of how the angel of the Lord appeared in a burning bush to deliver an important message to Moses. But there is a detail mentioned in the story that I have always found peculiar—the bush was burning, but it was *not* consumed:

> The angel of the LORD appeared to him in a blazing fire from the midst of a bush; and he looked, and behold, the bush was *burning with fire, yet the bush was not consumed.* (Exod. 3:2 NASB)

This Old Testament story has served as a mental picture for me of what it means to be a "bush" today. We are inhabited by God himself. He even speaks through us, making an appeal to the world to "be reconciled to God" (2 Cor. 5:20). But even though Christ lives in us and expresses himself through us, *he does not consume us.*

God is not trying to replace us. He already has—with a new self! Instead, God is embracing all that we are. It's all of him, and all of us, in a beautiful spiritual union. God does not consume us or circumvent us. He dwells within the midst of *all* that you call you!

As Paul put it to the Galatians, it is no longer us; it is Christ. But wait—it is indeed us, the *new* creation, living by faith in the one who loves us and gave himself for us (Gal. 2:20).

Smell the aroma of your union with Christ. Take it in. Know that you are one with Jesus. It is all of him, and it is all of you. And it is incredible!

OUR DEFAULT SETTING

When you purchase a computer, it comes with certain default settings. For example, if it's a Windows machine, it comes with Internet Explorer. Internet Explorer arrives with presets for colors, languages, fonts, toolbars, and many other things. These are default settings straight from the manufacturer.

Similarly, we humans show up on planet earth with some default settings. We are naturally bent toward sin. In fact, it's all we know—good-looking sin, bad-looking sin, and other varieties of sin. Life *in* the flesh is what we experience as our default setting. But at salvation, when the Spirit of Christ exchanges our old self for a new self and takes up residence within us, he gives us a new default setting. The most normal and natural thing for a Christian is to live uprightly. Conversely, the most unnatural and awkward thing for a Christian to do is sin. This is precisely why John writes the same thing twice in his epistle:

> No one who is born of God will continue to sin, because God's seed remains in them; *they cannot go on sinning*, because they have been born of God. (1 John 3:9)

> We know that anyone born of God *does not continue to sin*; the One who was born of God keeps them safe, and the evil one cannot harm them. (1 John 5:18)

Of course, we Christians *still* commit sins (1 John 2:1). This will be the case until we exit this world. But there's an important truth to be gleaned here: to "go on sinning" or to "continue to sin" as the everyday norm is no longer our default setting. Sin is now a most abnormal and unnatural thing for us as new creations in Christ. We are born of God, and everything in our spiritual DNA cries out against sin. Christ living through us is our new default setting.

ONE SPIRIT WITH HIM

So what does this life with Christ really look like? It looks like you, being yourself. It's not likely that someone will come running up to you saying, "Wow, you're so spiritual!" Sure, some around us may pick up on a peculiar hope or assurance we have within us. But we have this treasure in "jars of clay" so that the glory is of God and not of ourselves (2 Cor. 4:7).

It's not about trying to grab the attention of others in order to impress them. It's simply about living in the way we are designed to live—living *from* the life of Christ.

It's a *knowing*, not a feeling. It's not about pursuing some emotional high. Instead, it's about believing what we've heard. What have we heard? Heaven tells us that we are one spirit with Jesus Christ (1 Cor. 6:17). So our heavenly calling is to wake up every day and live as if this is 100 percent true, because it *is*!

We still have tough choices to make every day: forgiveness over bitterness; kindness over resentment; and patience over anger due to our unrealistic expectations. But in the end, it's about relationship, not performance. If we fix our eyes on a particular outcome, then we are worshiping the outcome, not Jesus. Heaven invites us to fix our eyes on Jesus, the author and perfecter of our faith (Heb. 12:2).

This is heaven's next message to us.

I have generously poured out my Spirit into your heart, and you have become an heir of a great hope and a great life in me. I have set my seal of ownership on you, and it is through my Spirit within that you cry out to me. My anointing remains in you forever and will teach you about all things. Through my Spirit, I will make known to you the glorious riches of your inheritance in me.

I am able to do more than you can possibly ask for or imagine, as it is my power that is at work within you to cause real change in your life. As you walk with me, you will indeed labor and strive, but it will be according to my power at work in you. I am the one who makes you stand firm, and I will carry you on to completion. It's you in me. And it's me in you. And it is life as I always intended.

Examine the fruit of my Spirit and see for yourself. Love, joy, peace, patience, kindness, gentleness, goodness, and self-control—these are born from a place of rest. My Spirit radiates through your life as you rest in the truth of my finished work. As you set your mind on all that I have done for you, you will exude and transmit my life to others. Expressing my life is your destiny.

Forces will tug at you to pull you away from this rest. Your own emotions will sometimes betray you as they are not aligned with my truth. You may feel dirty. You may feel distant from me. But I'm not inviting you to an emotional experience. I'm inviting you to truth, to a spiritual reality—your intimate union with me.

So come out to me, outside the realm of self-made religion, and walk in truth with me. I have promised never to leave you. The words I have spoken to you are like solid food that nourishes your entire being. Take in my living Word and be fed. I promise you will not be disappointed.

I love you.

Jesus

Awakening TO HEAVEN

Thank you, Jesus, for speaking words of life to me. No matter what ups and downs I may experience from day to day, you are my constant. You are my stability and strength. I am forever grateful for your love that never fades, your forgiveness that never ends, and your life that never fails to sustain me. I am convinced that you are a God of your word. You are always with me. You are always in me, offering your counsel and comfort. And you will complete this incredible work that you have begun in me. I am so thankful to

be a partaker of your divine nature here and now, when I need you the most.
I love you, Jesus.

Heaven Speaks inspired by Romans 5:5; 6:5; 8:5–6; 11, 15; 10:11; Galatians 3:29; 4:7; 5:22–23; 2 Corinthians 1:22; 2:15; 1 John 2:20, 27; Colossians 1:27, 29; Ephesians 1:18–19; 3:16, 20; 4:14; Philippians 1:6; 2:13; 2 Thessalonians 3:3; John 8:32; 15:5; 17:22–23; Hebrews 4:10; 13:5, 13; 1 Corinthians 6:17; 1 Peter 2:2; Isaiah 28:16.

17

I remember as a young Christian sitting and listening to many altar calls and "rededicate yourself" sermons. Time and time again, the speaker would exhort us to be salt and light in this world. He would tell us to do more for those around us. He would encourage us to spend more time in the Word, to share Christ more with others, and to plug in and serve more at church.

More. More. More.

Loving others, reading the Word, and sharing Christ—these are all good things. But I remember walking away from those "motivational" talks with a sense of distance from God, a sense that I was currently not doing enough to be close to him. Closeness was always around the next corner. And in all of this, the implication was that *closeness comes through doing.*

That's backwards.

The good news of Christianity is that on the first day of our relationship with Jesus Christ (at salvation), we are as close to him as we will ever be. Yes, we get to know Christ more over time. But we are raised and seated right next to him (Eph. 2:6) and one spirit with him (1 Cor. 6:17) on the day we first believe. We cannot get any closer to Jesus than we already are.

Once we acknowledge this union with Jesus, our motivation for every action taken in life changes. We are no longer doing to be close; instead, we are acting out of a closeness we already enjoy. This is what it means to smell the fragrant aroma of Christ.

CONNECTING THE DOTS

How does this radical, spiritual union with Jesus Christ affect the way we think about everyday relationship with God?

First, it means that our elementary knowledge of God can be replaced by a more mature understanding of him. God is not up in heaven waiting for us to place our long-distance phone call to him for help. He doesn't soar down out of heaven to stand beside us and help us through our trouble. It's better than that:

Therefore, my brethren, you also were made to die to the Law through the body of Christ, so that you might be *joined to another, to Him who was raised* from the dead, in order that we might bear fruit for God. (Rom. 7:4 NASB)

The one who joins himself to the Lord is *one spirit with Him*. (1 Cor. 6:17 NASB)

Examine yourselves to see whether you are in the faith; test yourselves. Do you not realize that *Christ Jesus is in you*—unless, of course, you fail the test? (2 Cor. 13:5)

Christ is not a far-off Someone we call upon now and then. Instead, he has raised us up with him and seated us in heaven alongside him. We are in two places at once—physically here on earth and spiritually seated with him in heaven (Eph. 2:6).

Second, it means that we don't have to go shopping for more of Jesus. You know what I mean. Lots of Christians seem to be on a hunt to get more of God in their lives. But as we have our spiritual senses awakened to the Jesus we already possess, the search comes to an end. We have everything we need:

Seeing that His divine power has granted to us *everything pertaining to life and godliness*, through the true knowledge of Him who called us by His own glory and excellence. (2 Pet. 1:3 NASB)

The greatest discovery we can make about this Christ-life within us is that we now possess all the qualities we need for any and every aspect of life. Take love, for example. Do you believe you need to have more love for others, or have you realized that the love of God himself has been poured out in your heart through God's Spirit (Rom. 5:5)? One belief system leads to *trying* to obtain more love and *trying* to be more loving. The other involves acknowledging that God has already re-created you as a loving person by nature. Did you catch that? By *nature*. This means we don't have to wait for God to zap us with more love. Instead, we are to count ourselves as dead to sin and alive to God, a God who *is* love. We are alive to love. We are inhabited by love. And that love is the person of Christ.

Lastly, our union with Jesus Christ means that our deepest needs are met in him and by him. Let's face it: there's not a soul on this planet who can really meet our needs. There is only One who can.

And my God will meet all your needs according to the riches of his glory in Christ Jesus. (Phil. 4:19)

So when we look to the church community to meet our needs, we will inevitably be disappointed.

That's looking to the creation rather than the Creator. It's the same in marriage. The Bible never tells us to look to our spouse for our needs to be met. That too will result in disappointment. Our spouse is the creation, not the Creator.

When we angle our soul mirror toward those around us, we will certainly be frustrated in seeking to meet our needs. The error lies in the angling of the mirror. We're designed to angle our soul toward heaven, where we are spiritually seated with Christ. We're designed to receive the life we need from Christ himself.

An Ancient Plan B

God promised Abraham that he would have a son. But after months and years had passed, Abraham and his wife, Sarah, started to worry. They were getting older and wondered when and how God would ever come through on his promise.

One day Sarah suggested that Abraham take matters into his own hands. Her idea was for Abraham to sleep with Hagar, Sarah's maid. Then Hagar could have his child, but the child would technically still belong to Sarah. This would be a creative way for them to "help" God come through. Surely God would honor their efforts!

In the midst of his panic over not having a son yet, Abraham gave in to Sarah's idea and conceived a child with Hagar. Ishmael was the product of Abraham's unbelief, and some quite troublesome circumstances in Israel's history eventually came about through Ishmael's descendants.

To some people, Sarah's motives might have looked good. She was willing to allow another woman to bear a child for her. She was doing it all in the name of helping God. What greater cause is there, right? Wrong. God simply doesn't honor this sort of "help" when he has provided another way through his promises.

It's the same for us today, on this side of the cross. It's not our job to "help God" produce fruit in our lives. It's not my efforts plus God's efforts. Just as Sarah was one day to bear the promised son, Isaac, we are designed to bear the promised fruit of God's Spirit. As Jesus himself explains, we are not the vine. We are merely the branches (John 15:5).

GOD'S FEDEX ROUTE

I grew up on a horse farm in a small town called Warrenton, Virginia. To this day, my mother lives only fifteen minutes away in a town called Gaines-ville. And my brother Will still lives in Warrenton and works as a real estate agent. Because of the nature of Will's work, he's always shipping paperwork via FedEx to clients all over the northern Virginia area. Consequently, Will's email inbox is filled with tracking numbers and links to routing information.

Will has learned a lot about FedEx and how they operate. FedEx utilizes certain cities as hubs, and this means that packages sometimes travel to their destination via some puzzling routes. For instance, if Will wants to send a package from Warrenton to my mother's house in Gainesville, FedEx may route that package from Warrenton, VA, to Fredericksburg, VA, to Indianapolis, IN, to Dulles, VA, to Herndon, VA, and then finally to Gainesville, VA.

Wow! Talk about a roundabout route! Even though a person can get in the car and drive that package from Warrenton to Gainesville in fifteen minutes or less, FedEx may choose what seems to us a very unusual path.

When I heard about the methods employed by FedEx, I thought of the "growth which is from God" (Col. 2:19 NASB). We don't always understand where the events in our lives are taking us or what God is doing in the midst of them all. The route God takes us on may seem as though it makes no sense at times. We may feel stalled or stuck, wondering why there seems to be no "progress" (however we might measure that!). But this we can know for sure: we are predestined to arrive at conformity to Christ's image (Rom. 8:29), via one route or another. The Person who began this trip with us will carry us on to completion (Phil. 1:6). And no matter what the route, God is always on time!

A destiny has been set before us, and our growth is a sure thing. Heaven wants us to know this.

HEAVEN SPEAKS

I don't want you tossed back and forth by every wind of teaching that comes your way. I want you to steadily grow and be built up into maturity in me. Just as you received me, continue to live in me, rooted and grounded in me and strengthened in your faith, overflowing in thankfulness to me—not because I require your thanks but because you are designed to live in gratefulness. It is both healthy and natural for the creation to look to the Creator and give thanks to me for all.

I have called you into fellowship with me, and I will sanctify you through and through so that your spirit, soul, and body are all set apart and blameless at my coming. My Spirit is the deposit, your guarantee that all of this will happen.

You will know both the fellowship of my sufferings and the power of my resurrection life. Know that you are being transformed into my image with a glory that comes only from my Spirit. Though physically you are wasting away, inwardly you are being renewed each day. And the afflictions you bear now do not compare to the glory I am working in you. So fix your eyes on what is invisible and eternal, for that is what matters most. I love you, and I'm so enjoying this journey with you.

Jesus

Awakening TO HEAVEN

Thank you, Jesus, that I need not wander into worry about my growth and my future. Thank you for promising to carry me through to maturity, conforming me to your image and your glory. I am willing to know your sufferings so that I may also know the power of your resurrection life in me. You alone meet my deepest needs. You are my steadfast anchor, my great hope in a sea of trouble. You are my everything.

I love you, Jesus.

Heaven Speaks inspired by Ephesians 1:14; 4:14; 5:20; Colossians 1:15; 2:6–7; 1 Thessalonians 5:18, 23; Romans 1:25; 8:18; 2 Timothy 2:13; 1 Corinthians 1:9; 2 Corinthians 1:22; 3:18; 4:16–18; Philippians 3:10–11.

TASTE
THE GOODNESS
OF THE LORD

Taste and see that the
LORD is good;
blessed is the one who
takes refuge in him.

Psalm 34:8

18

Steve walked up to me at the local coffee shop with a sheepish look about him.

"I'm sorry to bother you, but I wondered if I might talk to you for a second."

"Sure, Steve, what's up?" I said.

"Well, I've got a big decision ahead of me, and I've prayed about it over and over, and I just can't seem to find God's will."

"What decision is it?" I asked.

"I've got three job offers—one in Abilene, one in Amarillo, and one in Dallas. They all seem like good opportunities, but I just don't want to miss out on God's best. So I'm kinda stuck. I don't feel like I can choose *any* of them without knowing what he wants me to do."

"Ah, I see," I said. "Yeah, that's a pretty common problem for many of us Christians, especially those of us who are young like you and have lots of big decisions ahead."

"Yeah, so what would you do?" he asked, hoping I would solve his problem.

"Steve, when I was your age, I struggled with the very same thing, over and over, with decision after decision. I'd freeze up and not know what to do. I'd pray again and again and hear nothing. Then I'd wonder if it was something I was doing wrong that caused me to not be able to hear God's voice telling me what to do."

"That's it!" Steve said. "That's exactly what I feel like."

"Well, Steve, through it all, here's what I learned. It's not about being in Amarillo; it's about being in Christ. It's not about being in Abilene; it's about being in God's Spirit. And it's not about being in Dallas; it's about being in Jesus.

"Not once does the Bible tell us to wait on God for secret messages about which job to take or which cereal to eat in the morning. What we find is that God's will is much bigger than that. It's so big that we can't miss it. God's will is that we have relationship with him, talk with him, and bear his fruit. You can bear his fruit in Amarillo, Abilene, or Dallas. God is behind all three doors. He just wants to be life to us! That's his will."

Steve paused to consider what I'd said. Then he looked at me and asked, "So . . . the search is over?"

"Yes," I said, "Jesus tells us that if we eat and drink of him, we will never hunger or thirst again. The search *is* over, because we have *him*."

Within forty-eight hours, Steve had picked the job offer he was most excited about and was packing up to move. On his way out of town, he dropped off a note to me that read, "Thank you so much for helping me see God's will for my life—Jesus! I never realized it could be that simple."

BULL'S-EYE BELIEFS

Steve is not alone. The idea that we can miss out on God's "secret" will for our lives and be doomed to a lesser existence is a popular notion that has struck fear in the hearts of many Christians today. Essentially, it is a challenge to the goodness of the Lord. We will never "taste and see that the LORD is good" (Ps. 34:8) as long as we are afraid that he might punish us with a hopeless future (or a future with less hope!) because we failed to choose what he had secretly planned for us as the "God option."

If you're not familiar with this popular teaching, here's more or less how it goes. God has a perfect will, and that's like the center of a target, the bull's-eye. Then God has a permissive will, and that's like the rings just outside the bull's-eye. Then, lastly, there's the "entirely out of God's will" zone, which is like an outer ring of darkness.

You don't want to be out there.

Your job is to continually hit the bull's-eye throughout your life. Listen carefully, and you'll always make the right decisions—the right house, the right spouse, the right job, the right church. It'll all be smooth sailing if you just follow God's leading. He'll tell you just what to do. And if you can't hear his will very clearly, it's probably because there are some unconfessed sins in your life. Get those cleared up, and you'll be able to hear again!

This type of belief system is dangerous. I have seen it absolutely paralyze people. Some Christians are stuck like a deer in the headlights, not making a move until they hear from God. Others made a move long ago when they thought they heard from God, and now they're stuck in an incredibly difficult consequence and wondering, "How did God let this happen? I did exactly as he told me!"

Still others feel like they haven't heard from God concerning his will in years. "What's wrong with me?" they begin thinking. "Maybe I do have some unconfessed sins in my life, but I think I've confessed them all. Did I miss one?" Then they start trying to connect the dots between their current circumstances and past actions, trying to figure out what they did wrong that made God go silent on them. At this point, they stop believing in the effects of the cross and start believing in a Christian karma of sorts, retribution from almighty God.

The Truth about God's Will

So why is all of this wrong? For starters, the Scriptures never once speak of God's will as something that we go in and out of like a revolving door. A quick survey of the New Testament reveals that God's will is that we bear much fruit (John 15:8); that we pray without ceasing and give thanks (1 Thess. 5:17–18); that the gospel be extended to the Gentiles, not just the Jews (Eph. 1:11–13; 2:11–13); and that the gospel be proclaimed throughout all the earth (Col. 1:23; 2 Pet. 3:9). That's God's will, plain and simple. And that's the goodness of the Lord.

Consider, for example, the marriage decision. Paul's letter to the Corinthians reveals he has the right to "take a believing wife along" (1 Cor. 9:5). But then what does Paul decide? Perhaps because of dangers in the early church, Paul decides to remain single. He has the right to be married, but he doesn't exercise that right. Do you see the freedom in this?

We see something similar with regard to travel plans. Paul tells the Romans that he has planned many times to visit them but thus far has been prevented (Rom. 1:13). Can you believe that Paul, the apostle Paul, actually made plans that were prevented? That he didn't have a crystal ball enabling him to see into the future but actually got caught wasting time on plans that never came to fruition? Yes, even the apostle Paul lived in the dark on many things.

CHASING RIGHTEOUSNESS

Whether we realize it or not, this perpetual pursuit of God's perfect will is ultimately about us trying to stay right with God. The Bible calls this "righteousness." But righteousness is not gained through finding and doing a secret list of things that God has picked. Our righteousness comes from the death and resurrection of Christ, nowhere else. And once we take hold of that righteousness and are awakened to its sufficiency, we no longer need to be trapped in the bottomless pit of "finding God's will for our life."

Admittedly, this freedom is uncomfortable at first. But it ultimately breeds sound thinking, responsible choices, and a big God who is behind every door in life. This helps us awaken to God's grace in every circumstance and taste the goodness of our Lord.

This is the liberty heaven wants us to know.

My new way means you experience the liberty of my Spirit. I have not given you a spirit of fear but a sound mind in me. Do not be afraid of missing Father's best, as if it were a set of mysterious plans that you must somehow find. Father's will is me. Father's will is that you express my life. He simply desires for you to choose me in every moment, bearing my fruit. In so doing, you fulfill Father's will for your life.

I have placed my very desires within your heart and mind, and I have vowed to be with you now and for eternity. You belong to me and know me instinctively. You need not search for me and my will as if I am far off. Through my new way, I have made you close. I am the support beneath you, and I go before you into battle. I am one spirit with you, always. This is my covenant promise to you.

My Spirit assures you, again and again, that you are born of me. You are a child of my resurrection. Knowing me is your prized possession. Expressing me is your one and only ministry. Listen to my Word and my Spirit as I reveal to you the truths of my new way. Talk with me and give thanks for all I have given you. In this way, you fulfill Father's will for your life.

Taste my goodness, and know that I love you.

Jesus

Awakening TO HEAVEN

Thank you, Jesus, that I don't have to go searching in the dark for your will. You have revealed your will so clearly to me. You wanted to save me, and you did. Now you want relationship with me—to counsel me, mold me, and shape me. Your will is that I exude you, bearing much fruit in this life. No matter where I go and no matter what I do, there you are with me. Somehow, even in my darkest hour when I have made foolish choices, you are with me and work it for my good. Thank you, Jesus, for being God's will in my life.

I love you too.

Heaven Speaks inspired by 2 Corinthians 3:17; 5:18; Galatians 2:4; 2 Timothy 1:7; John 15:8–9; Hebrews 6:5, 13–19; 8:10–11; 1 Peter 2:9; Jeremiah 29:13; 31:34; Colossians 1:17, 22; Philippians 3:8; 4:13; 1 Corinthians 2:13; 6:17; Romans 8:16; Luke 20:36; 2 Peter 1:4; 1 Thessalonians 5:17–18; Psalm 34:8.

19

If you need something examined for authenticity, Steve Cain is your guy. For over two decades, Steve has served as one of the world's foremost experts in examining questionable documents and evidence. He's been employed by the United States Department of Justice, the Federal Bureau of Investigation, the Drug Enforcement Agency, the United States Secret Service, and the Internal Revenue Service. Steve has a trained eye and can tell you whether something is real or fake.

What's Steve's secret to being so good at it? It has everything to do with how well he knows the real thing. He can't possibly study every type of fraudulent document out there. Instead, he gets to know what authenticity looks like. In contrast, everything else just looks a bit "off."

Similarly, we Christians can expect all kinds of questionable, fraudulent thoughts to be tossed our way. Many of these thoughts may even masquerade as being from God himself. The only way we can tell the difference, identifying a counterfeit, is to get to know the real thing, tasting the goodness of the Lord. Once we see what truth is supposed to look like—our total forgiveness, our freedom from the law, our new identity in Christ, and the security of his presence within us—everything else just looks a bit "off."

A New Motivation

Heaven's new covenant is authentic Christianity. It's a perfect expression of the goodness of the Lord, and it's no counterfeit. The results of God's new way are unmistakable. It inspires us to act from a heavenly, heartfelt motive rather than from an earthly guilt or sense of obligation.

A shift in focus brings this new motivation. In being forgiven completely, we need not focus on our sins. In being accepted unconditionally by God's grace, we need not focus on our performance. In becoming new creations, we need not get on the treadmill of pursuing religious righteousness. In being united with Christ, we need not be consumed with pleading and begging for more of his presence.

No, it's all been taken care of, and the results of this new covenant are dramatic. We are fixed firmly to heaven. And we can finally taste the goodness of the Lord!

GAUGING HIS GOODNESS

Recently, I was in a store picking up some groceries for our family when I found myself in the toy aisle. I stopped for a minute to examine the toys, thinking my four-year-old son, Gavin, might enjoy a surprise. After a bit of careful consideration, I tossed one in my cart—a bright red sports car with doors that opened, a trunk that opened, and a transparent rear panel so you could see the engine inside. It had more features than the other vehicles, and I knew he'd love it!

When I got home and presented the surprise gift to Gavin, it was I who was more surprised than Gavin.

"What else did they have there?" Gavin asked.

A bit taken aback, I answered, "Well, they had little motorcycles and helicopters and other cars too, but this one was the biggest and has doors and a trunk that open. The others didn't open, and on this one you can see the engine too."

"Well, what other colors did they have?" he asked.

Not sure where this was going, I revealed, "They had a silver one and this red one, but I knew red was your favorite."

"Cool," he said. "Well, I do like this one the best. Thanks, Daddy!"

My heart melted upon hearing his decision to embrace the new red sports car. At first, I wasn't certain where things were headed! Would he like my choice? Would he be satisfied? It turns out he was just doing a bit of research and wanted to make sure he was getting the very best option available.

That event makes me laugh every time I think about it. Like father, like son, I guess. I do the same thing—I research and analyze my options before making a purchase, whether big or small. Maybe it's just a human thing for many of us. We want to be absolutely certain that we got the very best deal we could find.

It's the same when it comes to spiritual truth. It's important for us to know that we have the best thing out there. But if we haven't yet awakened to heaven's new way of grace, it's very difficult to pass off Christianity as the best thing going. We simply can't taste the goodness of the Lord today apart from the new covenant. Instead, we are left to wallow in our own thoughts and feelings about God to determine if he is good and to what degree.

It's the new covenant that *defines* the goodness of the Lord for us today. Through the new covenant, his goodness is defined in exact spiritual terms, not by soulish emotions.

HEAVEN ON EARTH

First, *our freedom from the law* translates into a no-strings-attached, total acceptance that we are anchored to through Christ. This freedom from the law means that we need not walk on eggshells with the Lord. We can move forward confidently, knowing that we are loved with an unshakable, unbreakable love purchased through blood.

Second, we taste the goodness of the Lord in the new covenant as heaven has bestowed on us *a new identity*, making us clean and close to God. We are heavenly at the core. Our righteousness is not some positional status God has given us while we actually remain dirty and distant. No, God has actually cleansed us and made us new. He has given us a place of honor in his family by exchanging our old spiritual DNA for a new self. We are now literally and actually partakers of his divine nature (2 Cor. 5:17; Col. 3:10; 2 Pet. 1:4).

Third, *our new covenant forgiveness* is an incredible demonstration of the Lord's goodness toward us. While the forgiveness of old involved animal sacrifices once a year, the new covenant forgiveness we now enjoy is very different. Jesus Christ is not up in heaven dying again and again, and therefore, we are not being forgiven progressively. Instead, the sin issue is now over. Christ is seated in heaven at

God's right hand, and his work is finished. This means we are completely forgiven and cleansed people, entirely reconciled to God.

Lastly, the new covenant announcement is that God has given us *his divine life*. Life has been restored to the place formerly housing death. When our human spirit was exchanged, old for new, we were filled with God's Spirit and sealed by him until Christ's return (Eph. 1:13–14). His presence in us is for here and now, and his presence is for the eternity we already participate in.

Freedom, identity, forgiveness, and life—these make up heaven's new way. Each enables us to taste the goodness of the Lord in a special way. Each awakens our spiritual senses to a heaven that is *now*.

HEAVEN SPEAKS

I invite you to feast on the goodness of my new covenant. Through it, I have shown you a simple, singular focus—me. I am your once for all sacrifice for sins. I am your freedom from the law. And I am your source for life. Taste and see that I am good, and enjoy my heavenly promises now and forevermore.

I love you more than you can possibly imagine.

Jesus

Awakening TO HEAVEN

My Jesus, you've changed how I look at myself, how I look at others, and how I see you. Thank you for forgiving me once for all. Thank you for freeing me from the impossible standard of the law. Thank you for giving me a brand-new identity. But most of all, thank you for the gift of your life. You are so incredibly good to me, and I will love you all the days of my life.

Heaven Speaks inspired by John 6:35, 56; Hebrews 7:27; 12:2; 1 Peter 3:18; Romans 6:7, 10, 14; 7:6; Colossians 3:4; Psalm 34:8; 2 Peter 1:4; Ephesians 3:19.

STUDY QUESTIONS

Awaken!

1. Of the five spiritual senses, which are you most excited to have awakened? Why is that one so special to you?

2. What do you believe it means to "make every *effort* to enter God's *rest*" (Heb. 4:11)?

FEEL the Freedom of Grace

1. Why do you think it's so difficult for us to trust in God's grace for anything beyond salvation?

2. *Grace* is a common buzzword these days. Do you think our understanding of God's grace has fallen short? If so, how?

3. At the heart of the new covenant is God's faithfulness to himself. How does this affect your view of salvation and life in Christ?

4. Can you relate to the story about Prohibition in the United States? In what ways has being under laws or rules excited sin in your life?

5. How does understanding the old covenant context of Jesus's harsh teachings (cut off your hand, be perfect, sell everything, etc.) help you feel the freedom of grace on this side of the cross?

6. The prisoners of Shawshank prison were uncomfortable with freedom after their release. In what ways do you think our freedom in Christ can be uncomfortable at first?

HEAR THE SPIRIT BEARING WITNESS

1. We are who we are by birth, *not* by what we do. How does this help you hear the Spirit bearing witness to your true identity as a child of God?

2. What is the flesh? How might the realization that the struggle is between God's Spirit and

the flesh (Gal. 5:17) change the way you approach the battle?

3. Understanding that a power called *sin* can offer sinful thoughts to our minds at any time is a startling revelation for many. But how is it also a heavenly call to reinterpret the way we view ourselves and our thinking?

4. Do you find it helpful to see that we have a spirit *and* a soul? How does this perspective help explain our 100 percent righteous condition in Christ despite the ongoing renewal of the mind?

5. In what ways have you based your theology on the roller coaster of your soul when heaven calls us to worship God in *spirit* and in truth?

SEE THE FINISHED WORK OF JESUS

1. Will Jesus ever die for our sins again? Given God's blood economy for sins, what does this mean for the type of forgiveness you now have?

2. How does the image of Jesus relaxing in a seated position at our Father's right hand help you understand the nature of your forgiveness?

3. How does our total forgiveness factor in at Christ's return? Do you believe that God will remember our sins on judgment day? Why or why not?

4. In what way can 1 John 1:9 be misunderstood as a "bar of soap" cleanser for the Christian? What is this passage really about in context?

5. If we don't have to ask for forgiveness each time we sin, what should we do when we sin? How does the "stop, drop, and roll" fire analogy help explain this?

6. Take a minute to browse the "Big Picture" list of forgiveness passages near the end of chapter 13. Do you think God was naïve in forgiving us this way, with no strings attached? How might realizing our permanently clean state before him affect the way we think and act on a daily basis?

SMELL THE FRAGRANT AROMA OF CHRIST

1. At any point in your life, could you relate to Michael, who had a surface-level understanding of Christianity but didn't really know what it meant to have Christ's *life* in him?

2. At Christmas, we celebrate the incarnation of Christ—Jesus coming to earth in human flesh. How might *our own compatibility* with the life of Christ now residing in us give us even more appreciation as we celebrate Christmas?

3. How is Christ living *through* us different from us merely living *for* Christ?

4. "All of God and none of us"—how does this idea fall short, and how does our union with Christ explain things better?

5. What would you say to someone who seems fearful of "surrendering" to Christ living through them because they are afraid of "God's will" for their life?

TASTE THE GOODNESS OF THE LORD

1. If someone asked you to explain the new covenant in your own words, what would you say it's all about?

2. How does heaven's new way change the way you look at yourself? your sins? your relationship with God?

3. In what ways have you been awakened to the wonders of God's grace? In what ways might you need to be further awakened to his goodness?

MY FIVE SPIRITUAL SENSES

Sense 1: **FEEL** the Freedom of Grace

- *I am dead to the law.* (Rom. 7:4, 6; Gal. 2:19)
- *I am not under the law.* (Rom. 6:14; Gal. 5:18)
- *I am not supervised by the law.* (Gal. 3:25)
- *The requirements of the law have been fully met in me.* (Rom. 8:3–4)
- *Christ is the end of the law for me.* (Rom. 10:4)
- *I serve in God's new way, led by his Spirit.* (Rom. 7:6; Gal. 5:18)

Sense 2: **HEAR** the Spirit Bearing Witness

- *My old self is dead, buried, and gone.* (Rom. 6:6–7; Gal. 2:20)
- *I am dead to sin and alive to God.* (Rom. 6:11)

- *I am a new creation re-created in Christ Jesus.* (2 Cor. 5:17; Eph. 2:10)
- *The struggle is against the flesh and sin, not against myself.* (Rom. 7:17, 20; Eph. 6:12)
- *I am more than a conqueror through Jesus Christ.* (Rom. 8:37)

SENSE 3: SEE THE FINISHED WORK OF JESUS

- *I have been forgiven and cleansed once for all.* (Heb. 9:28; 10:2)
- *By one sacrifice I have been made perfect forever.* (Heb. 10:14)
- *I have been made holy through Jesus's sacrifice once for all.* (Heb. 10:10)
- *I have been reconciled to God.* (Eph. 2:16; Col. 1:22)
- *I have fellowship with God.* (1 Cor. 1:9; 1 John 1:3)
- *My totally forgiven state is a powerful inspiration to forgive others.* (Eph. 4:32; Col. 3:13)

SENSE 4: SMELL THE FRAGRANT AROMA OF CHRIST

- *Having eternal life means having Christ's life.* (John 17:3; 1 John 5:12)

- *Christ literally and actually lives in me.* (2 Cor. 13:5; Gal. 2:20)
- *It is all of him and all of me in union together.* (Rom. 6:5; 1 Cor. 6:17)
- *God is at work in me, carrying his work to completion.* (Phil. 1:6; 2:13)

Sense 5: TASTE the Goodness of the Lord

- *The Lord's will is that I bear his fruit.* (John 15:8)
- *The Lord's will is that I talk to him and give thanks to him.* (1 Thess. 5:17–18)
- *The Lord forgave me, canceled my debt, and made me alive.* (Col. 2:13–14)
- *The Lord demonstrates his love for me in his new covenant.* (Rom. 5:8; 2 Cor. 3:6)

ACKNOWLEDGMENTS

First, I want to thank my wife, Katharine, and my son, Gavin, for their love and support while I was writing this book. I want to thank my mother, Leslie Farley, for her encouragement to me over the years. I am also blessed to have the love and support of Doug and Maurita Hayhoe. A special thank-you goes to Andrea Heinecke at Alive Communications. I want to express my appreciation to Rob Jackson at Extra Credit Projects for the design of the book cover. And I want to thank Baker Books for partnering with me in this book ministry. In particular, I'd like to acknowledge Robert Hosack, Wendy Wetzel, Michael Cook, Ruth Anderson, David Lewis, Paula Gibson, and Erin Bartels.

I am so grateful to the leadership and members of Ecclesia for their support. In particular, I want to thank Chip Polk, Rex Kennedy, Steven Bailey, Joshua Sills, Jordan Polk, Jill Mull, and Kimberly Martin.

Finally, I want to thank you, the reader. If you enjoyed this book, consider passing it on to someone who is dear to your heart.

Andrew Farley is senior pastor of Ecclesia, an evangelical church that has resided on the high plains of West Texas for more than fifty-five years, and a bestselling author of several books, including *The Naked Gospel* and *God without Religion*. Andrew serves as a faculty adviser for InterVarsity Christian Fellowship and frequently speaks at churches and university groups around the United States and in Canada. Andrew is also a professor of applied linguistics at Texas Tech University in West Texas, where he lives with his wife, Katharine, and their son, Gavin. For more information, please visit Andrew Farley.org.

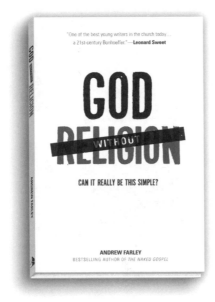

AndrewFarley.org

At Andrew's website, you'll also find powerful resources to share with your church, Sunday school class, or small group, including:

- Hundreds of video and audio messages
- Submit your own question
- Group study questions
- New book updates
- Andrew's blog
- Free sample chapters

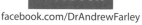